GLUE SNIFFING AND VOLATILE SUBSTANCE ABUSE

To all those who practice
caring for children and
young people.

And I looked, and behold a pale horse:

and his name that sat on him was Death

and Hell followed him.

(Apocalypse, 6.8)

Glue Sniffing and Volatile Substance Abuse

Case Studies of Children and Young Adults

DENIS O'CONNOR
The School of Education,
University of Newcastle upon Tyne

Gower

Published by
Gower Publishing Company Limited,
Gower House, Croft Road, Aldershot, Hampshire GU11 3HR, England
and
Gower Publishing Company,
Old Post Road, Brookfield, Vermont 05036, U.S.A.

Reprinted 1984 (twice), 1985, 1986

British Library Cataloguing in Publication Data

O'Connor, Denis
    Glue sniffing and volatile substance abuse.
    1. Solvent abuse—Study and teaching
    I. Title
    613.813   HV5822.S65

Library of Congress Cataloging in Publication Data

O'Connor, Denis, 1934-
    Glue sniffing and volatile substance abuse.
    Includes bibliographical references.
    1. Glue-sniffing. 2. Glue-sniffing—Treatment.
    3. Youth—Substance use. I. Title.
    HV5822.G4025 1983   362.2'9   83-16464

    ISBN 0 566 00641 3

Printed in Great Britain by Biddles Ltd, Guildford, Surrey

CONTENTS

Initial involvement. Defining and describing the
problems. Setting up the University Counselling
Clinic. Aims of the Study. Researching effective
treatments. Treatment for symptoms. Treatment
for sniffers. The importance of subjective
factors.

Historical perspectives on sniffing. Evidence
from different parts of the world. Sniffing as a
recreational activity. Early use of ether,
chloroform and a laughing gas (nitrous oxide) at
parties. Glue sniffing by schoolchildren. Solvent
abuse in Lanarkshire, Scotland. Statistics
indicating geographical areas of UK requesting
information. Incidents of abuse. Police referrals
to social services (CYP's). The method of abuse.
Products abused. Patterns of use.

Deaths. A tragic case. The physical effects:
physical signs, personal signs. Body damage
effects. The social ill effects. Psychological
damage.

4 CAUSES AND MOTIVATIONS

5 MANAGEMENT

6 TREATMENT

7 OVERALL VIEW

8 POSTSCRIPT

9 REFERENCES

FIGURES

FOREWORD

It is not often that one can introduce an academic colleague (and friend) as someone who has appeared on Nationwide, Horizon and the Jimmy Young show. That the underlying reason for Denis O'Connor's appearances on such programmes is the phenomenon of glue sniffing and solvent abuse amongst children and adolescents indicates society's concern for the problem.

A frightening aspect of glue sniffing is the lack of support services for the victims. There is, currently, little professional help available, and it is a salutory lesson to remember that no child is immune whatever their background.

Denis O'Connor became interested in the problem almost accidentally in the course of his duties as a psychologist tutor at the University of Newcastle upon Tyne. His concern was such that he turned his professional and personal attention to those unfortunate young people with whom he came into contact. Since then, he has become, arguably, the country's leading authority on the treatment of glue sniffers and solvent abusers. His counselling clinic is renowned in the UK and is increasingly being recognised abroad.

There are few university lecturers who would work a seven hour Saturday in addition to their normal Monday to Friday job. There are even fewer who would do this without payment. Denis O'Connor does. His clinic is operated entirely without financial backing and formal support. The voluntary staff who assist him do so as a result of concern for, and appreciation of, the problem. Not least, perhaps, is a genuine respect and affection for their director.

In spite of the considerable demands made upon his time I am delighted that he has been able to produce this text which will illuminate a serious social problem area.

John McGregor McMaster

ACKNOWLEDGEMENTS

I wish to acknowledge the many people who have given willingly of their time and effort to support me in the preparation of this book.   I would like to especially thank the following persons by name without whose help this work would not have been possible:

    Sr. Marie Concepta
    Police Superintendent Rhona Cross, MBE,
    Police Sergeant Edna Weir
    Police Inspector L. Montague
    Peter Clark
    Olive Carrott
    John McGregor McMaster
    Ian Fairfax
    Peter Occleston

and the Counselling students who maintained the Clinic, in particular: Colin Finlay, Alan Galloway, Carey Walker, Alison Orton, Alan Feltoe, Graham Skirrey, George Neighbour, Howard Firth, Helen Fletcher, and Estelle Jones.

And finally in gratitude to my University for allowing me the freedom to pursue this research and to Gower for undertaking its publication.

                                    Denis O'Connor

PROLOGUE
First Contact

I waited looking out from behind the tall Georgian windows of the
Counselling Clinic for a long time before he eventually appeared.
Immediately I sensed uncertainty as realising he was late he hurriedly
crossed the park scanning the way ahead for our address.   He'd
probably only made up his mind to come at the last minute, I thought.
His mother had sounded nervous, a strident note in her voice
intensified by the telephone as she pleaded for an appointment.

'I was supposed to come at 2.00 o'clock', he began, gasping from his
recent exertions.   I looked him over as he stepped inside the building
and preceded me up the stairs.   A thin face, chin sores and blemish
marks on the cheeks showing red against the pallor, shoulders hunched
against the autumn chill in the inadequate jacket, mouth open breathing
altogether too heavily for the slight climb considering his tall slim
build.   It was Thursday afternoon in October 1979 and I was meeting my
first glue sniffer.

Quietly seated he told me of the events that had led him to me and
why he so desperately wanted treatment.   He had started sniffing glue
fumes approximately 18 months previously.   At first he'd enjoyed the
experience especially the wonderful dreams in which, he told me,
anything could come true.   It was about that time that he'd stopped
trying any more at school and spent as much time as he could glue
sniffing.   A few times the police caught him and he was forced under
threat of legal action against his mother to attend school but after
a while he drifted back to his old ways only this time he would go to
school first, get his attendance mark and then leave.   A lot of the
time he had sniffed in a small group of other boys sharing the glue
which they collectively bought or, as often happened, stolen from a
supermarket or DIY store.   Then he found it more convenient to sniff
alone although he knew this was dangerous since there would be no one
there to care for him if anything went wrong.   Sometimes he would
inhale the contents of a one litre tin to himself in one day, usually
it was 500 mls.   For weeks on end he sniffed every day, occasionally
he had a day or two when he did not sniff but these were infrequent.
One day he noticed how badly his hands trembled and it alarmed him
when he could not control them.   It was about that time that the pains
started.   Deep pains around the left temple and forehead and over the

the left eye.   Chest pains when he breathed and shooting pains in his
lower back.   Now and again after a sniffing session he could not
remember what had happened but suspected that he'd been unconscious for
a while.   All of this was bearable he told me but lately events had
taken a sinister turn depressing him so badly that he'd sometimes
started weeping uncontrollably.   His mother had begged him to seek help
and after trying half-heartedly elsewhere he had found his way to me.

'What is it', I asked him, 'that made you try to stop sniffing'?
He stared at me for some time before replying almost as if he wondered
whether it was worth the effort to try to convince yet another person.
He sighed, looked away from me and when he spoke it was in a hollow
tone of voice: It had happened one night after a lengthy sniffing
session in a graveyard, a favourite haunt of glue sniffers.   He could
not remember the time only that it was late.   He recalls sitting back
against a gravestone watching the clouds passing over the moon and
thinking that it was time to go home.   All at once a voice spoke to
him although he could not see anyone.   'Hello, I'm Pilsnor and I've
come to stay with you', the voice said.   Drowsily he clambered to his
feet and looked around him half expecting to see a fellow sniffer
possibly an acquaintance but there was no one there.   Not a little
frightened and suddenly sobering he hurried out of the churchyard
heading for home.   On reaching the bedroom he shared with his elder
brother he undressed quickly in the dark and slipped quietly into bed:
He was almost asleep when he was startled awake by the Voice: "It's
Pilsnor again, I'm watching you".   He must have screamed and yelled
out because the whole house was awakened and it was hours before
everybody settled down again.   He did not sleep at all that night.
It was only afterwards when he realised the full terror of it that he
understood why he had screamed, 'You see', he told me, 'the Voice was
in my head but wasn't any part of me'.

He described the Voice as male, deep and very gruff.   It frightened
him because it spoke without warning, telling him to do bad things.
He spoke of it as coming and going from somewhere in the back of his
head.

'You say the Voice can come without warning?' I asked gently probing
for a clearer perspective on his condition.   He shivered before
replying:

'When I sniff the glue I know the Voice will come but I don't know
when.   Suddenly it's there speaking to me.   I think that if I could
stop sniffing' he said, 'it would never come back but I've tried and
I can't', he slumped helplessly in the chair.   Slowly he raised his
head and told me what to him was apparently the most frightening
aspect of all.

'Just lately before the Voice goes it usually says something that
really gets to me as if it knows I can do nothing to stop it'.

'What's that?' I queried noticing that he was sweating.

'It says "We'll meet again, Anthony.   Remember you have a rendezvous
with Pilsnor" and I know that he means I've got to sniff again'.

'How long has this been going on?' I asked.

'About two months more or less' he told me, 'but there's more, and this is why I thought I'd come to see you today. 'You see the Voice has started saying the last few times that soon I'll be able to see him and I don't want to, I'm scared'.

I looked across my study at the worried looking young teenager and thought over what he had said over the last hour as I waited for him to stop crying.

From that day onwards I embarked upon a close study of what is commly called glue sniffing. In the course of this study I have met many young people struggling to escape their dependency on the kicks they get from these fumes. In the pages that follow there is an account of my own very special rendezvous with Pilsnor and his victims who like Anthony came to the Clinic and shared their sufferings with me.

1 INTRODUCTION

This book is about the noxious practice by young people of inhaling poisonous fumes from a number of products in everyday domestic and commercial use. It describes the findings from three years of clinical experience and research with over 500 school children and adolescents involved in this abuse. But it is essentially about the young people who inhale toxic vapours and the feelings they have about themselves as persons. 'Glue sniffer' and 'solvent abuser' are labels used for the convenience of assessment and diagnosis. These terms are suitable for statistical reports but tend to mask the fact that every so called sniffer has a unique personality of his or her own, lives within a special family, has friendship groups peculiar to his community, and has private hopes and wishes for his life. Many are still in their childhood years, some in late adolescence but they all, irrespective of age, want to escape for a variety of reasons from the ordinary routines of living to a chemically induced fantasy world. When intoxicated the young person usually experiences feelings of release from everyday stresses and strains. Drowsy feelings often give way to vivid hallucinations which realise the person's needs for emotional comfort and recreation through dreams of wish fulfilment or nightmares of excitement. The troubles which can develop from this abuse and the often dire consequences which follow prolonged exposure to toxic vapours is generally unsuspected until it is too late for the person to avoid suffering some ill effects.

The practice involves deliberately inhaling the fumes from glues and other products containing solvents for the immediate purpose of gaining a feeling of pleasure where everything feels good and looks good and where worries and problems tend to be diminished in rather a similar way to the early stages of intoxication from alcohol. It is a form of self-abuse which can have highly dangerous results for the young person, when it is indulged to extremes; the consequences have been in some cases quickly fatal, in others the damage to the major organs of the body such as heart, lungs, liver, kidneys and the brain can be a slow process of deteriorating health with the possibility of lethal outcomes ever present (Clark and Tinston, 1982)

While glue sniffing is the popular term used to describe this practice it is not really accurately descriptive of all the many related activities which are involved. There are a number of definitive reasons which seem to extend the meaning of the term far beyond 'glue sniffing'. For instance:

1. The practice is not confined simply to glues and adhesives but also refers to the deliberate inhalation of chemical fumes from a variety of substances which are in everyday domestic and industrial use. For example, the solvent in glue which has a disabling effect on the central nervous system of sniffers, is toluene, an aromatic hydrocarbon which is chemically related to benzene and which is also found in plastic cement, paints, paint lacquers and thinners. (see list in fig. 1.1).

2. It is the glue vapour which is not only sniffed through the nose but often inhaled deeply through the mouth. The glue itself is <u>not</u> inhaled although some young people have been found with smears of glue inside their nostrils and around their mouths.

3. Another of the related activities to which this practice refers is the drinking of solvents like paraffin and petrol usually by sucking the moisture from a rag saturated with the liquid. The solvents have also been added to alcoholic or soft drinks: for example, butane gas for cigarette lighters has been sprayed into drinks like lager and cola.

In view of the range of activities involved as indicated above it is more appropriate to refer to solvent abuse, or following Anderson et al, 1982, Volatile Substance Abuse, in order to indicate the comprehensive nature of the problems while at the same time recognising that the more popular term is glue sniffing.

The studies reported within this text are not characteristic of the usual research projects which Universities spawn. This one grew from a series of chance encounters unplanned and unsolicited. The outcome was for me the realisation that the seriousness of the problems merited not only further study but immediate help and supportive care for the young people and their families. It all really started with a series of chance incidents.

The first of these occurred in the autumn of 1978 when a mature student reading Counselling Studies began to research solvent abuse activities of young adolescents. I was appointed by the University to supervise her research but I knew nothing about the subject matter of the investigation. Some months later this student was unable to complete her work for reasons of ill health. Before leaving she asked if I would use her research notes to write an article publicising the dangers of deliberately inhaling solvent fumes. Eventually a short annotation was published (O'Connor, 1979) which outlined the activities involved and highlighted the potential health hazards arising from these indulgences. The outcome was startling and threatened to overwhelm my capacity to cope with the many requests for help which arose as a result.

Figure 1.1

VOLATILE SUBSTANCE ABUSE CHART

PRODUCT	VOLATILES	INTENDED USE
Glues	Toluene	Household repairs
Adhesives	N-Hexane	
Plastic Cement	Hexane	Model making and bonding plastic
	Acetone	
Fingernail	Acetone	Cosmetic use
Polish and		
Remover	Amyl Acetate	
Typing Eraser	Amyl Acetate	Correcting typing errors
Dyes: Clothing	Methylene	Dying fabrics etc
	Chloride	
Paint Thinners	Toluene	Thinning paint and varnish
	Ethyl Acetate	
	Cellosolve	
	Acetate	
Rubber solution	Benzene	Carpet fitting, moulding adhesive uses etc.
	Hexane	
	Chloroform	
Petrol	Benzene	Motor fuel, lighter fuel, degreasing etc.
Dry Cleaning	Carbon	Cleaning clothing.
Fluids	Tetrachloride	
	Trichloro-	
	ethane	
Aerosols:	Usually contain)	
Pain killer	Refrigerants)	Used for relieving muscular pain especially by sportsmen
Hair spray	and propellants)	Cosmetic uses
Damp start	in a mixture)	Quick drying agent for car distributors etc.
De-Icer	of volatile)	Used to remove frost and ice from car windows.
Gas lighter	hydrocarbons)	Filling cigarette lighters
fuel		

3

Car paints   under com-   )   Used for patching vehicle paintwork
Sealants   pression   )   Building repairs

Fig. 1.1

The events which followed reminded me of the student from whom this research had been inherited, 'Nobody seems to care', she said, 'The authorities regard the whole thing with a mixture of scepticism and humour. No one seems to want to become involved with the crazy kids who sniff glue'. During my initial involvement with solvent abuse practices I was forced to recognise again and again the grim reality of her statement.

I mmediately following the publication mentioned above I was faced with responding to the needs for treatment which solvent abuses had generated in the younger population, both in the local region of Tyneside and elsewhere in the United Kingdom. Adding to my problems still further were the surprising number of requests for information received from many different parts of the world (see fig. 1.2)

It appeared that a lot of people needed to refer to an authority on the subject and because of my article it was assumed that I was an expert in spite of the fact that I had never counselled a glue sniffer. It is true however that experience is an effective teacher. I was accustomed to receiving a limited number of referrals each month, four or five pupils with behaviour problems for counselling treatment. These cases were a useful way of training students in the methods and skills of counselling practice. Following the recognition of my interest in solvent abuse the number of referrals began to increase at an alarming rate, threatening to overwhelm all the clinical services we could offer. In view of this I decided to open the Counselling Clinic to the general public on Saturdays to provide a walk in facility especially for the reception and treatment of solvent abuse cases. Volunteers from the counselling students assisted me in providing this service which I expected would soon exhaust the need but subsequent events proved otherwise.

To date, July 1983, the Counselling Clinic continues to flourish and has also proved to be a source of information for many members of the child welfare and caring professions urgently seeking guidance on the subject of glue sniffing and solvent abuse. It has achieved wide recognition and popularity over the last four years in providing support and treatment for large numbers of young people and their families. Because of my experience in counselling solvent abusers I regularly receive requests to write and speak on this subject. It seems that the need for information on glue sniffing and solvent abuse appears to have intensified rather than abated over the years chiefly owing to factors such as the following:

1. Public alarm, often panic type responses, especially
    by parents to the unusual task of coping with the
    highly intoxicated behaviour of school children and
    adolescents.

2. The deaths and serious ill effects evidenced in a small
    number of cases which have usually been grossly over
    publicised in the news media.

VOLATILE SUBSTANCE ABUSE

Index of need for information about VSA as indicated by written
requests to the author following publication of a paper on gluesniffing
and solvent abuse, (O'Connor, 1979).

Period September 1979 to August 1980

Requests for Reprints of Article			Total 293
	NE Region*	UK except NE	Overseas
Written and telephone	186	63	44

Written requests
from UK:
Edinburgh, Glasgow, Dunfermline, Bristol,
Northamptonshire, Lancashire, Exeter, London,
Romford, Wolverhampton, Co. Antrim, Northern
Ireland.

Written requests
from Overseas:
Berlin, Munich, West Germany, Unterschrift,
Berlin; Gif-sur-Yvette, France; Lyon Cedex 2,
France; Stockholm, Sweden; Madrid, Spain;
Obranco mir 10, Czecholslovakia; Trinity College,
Dublin, Argentina, South Africa, USA; West
Virginia, Boston, Mississippi, Oklahoma, Michigan,
Florida, California, New York, Indiana,
Washington, Oregon, Maine, Texas, Alabama,
Seattle, Ohio, Maryland, Mexico, Canada:
Alberta, Ontario, Vancouver.

Requests to speak to professional groups in the region:

Police, Educational Psychologists, Psychiatrists, Medical Practitioners,
Social Workers, Residential Care Staff, Youth Workers, Nursing Staff,
Civil Service Manpower Service Commission, Headteachers, Teachers,
Hospital Staff, Counsellors, Educational Welfare Officers, Drug
Liaison Committee, Parent-Teacher Associations.

*Triangulated area: Ashington to Stockton to Carlisle.

Figure 1.2

3. The apparent inability of the caring professions to respond with appropriate strategies and remedies due mainly to the absence of helpful information and guidelines for caring.

4. The increasing numbers of young people who presented as being in need of management and treatment, for example as witnessed by Police referrals of sniffers to the Social Services through the Children and Young Persons' Act 1969.

5. Public disturbances requiring increased intervention by the Police following incidents in which sniffers appeared to be at risk of injury and/or were in danger of committing offences against the law.

6. The escalation of problems such as truancy and school refusal among pupils in large urban comprehensive schools. Many of these pupils spend their time inhaling solvents as an alternative to schooling.

7. The realisation by many responsible professional groups that solvent abuses by the young are more serious than the passing phase they were once thought to be. Contrary to earlier hopes, especially by those who advocated adopting a low profile approach (ISDD, 1980) echoes of which are still to be seen (Herzberg & Wolkind, 1983), there are still no signs of the practice disappearing.

In view of the urgency of such features I decided to investigate solvent abuse practices as far as my resources would allow with the purpose of exploring and defining the problem. It was hoped to provide answers to some vital questions for example:

1. What do glue sniffing practices actually involve?

2. What is the background to these practices?

3. What is already known about such problems?

4. Who are the sniffers and where do they come from?

5. What are the effects of glue sniffing?

6. How can young people suffering from glue sniffing practices best be helped?

7. What kind of advice and guidance on glue sniffing would be suitable for (a) parents, (b) members of the Caring Professions?

It was considered that to research answers to these questions would provide a basis of factual information essential to the development of responsible and caring attitudes to the subject. There had already been a lot of speculation which had led to the emergence of opposed points of view, namely:

That Glue Sniffing is dangerous and should be stopped.

That Glue Sniffing is not dangerous and should be ignored.

Rumours regarding the ill effects or lack of them, fuelled by wide media coverage, were rife and there existed too much confusion for any clear strategies to develop which would allay feelings of crisis in the adult population.

Further to the above points it became clear that research would have to be aimed at finding out exactly what was the nature and outcomes of glue sniffing practices which seemed to be such an ill defined area. It would be necessary to identify the significant psychological variables for a number of reasons:

1. To describe those signs which would lead to early detection and recognition which in turn would lead hopefully to effective handling of the treatment side.

2. To assess the effects of the chemical fumes on behaviour.

3. To marshall the available data, with the purpose of providing guidelines on management and treatment strategies.

The first task was to describe with accurate detail what exactly goes on when a group of individuals begin a 'glue sniffing' session.

At the time I began to study the problem in 1979 there were many assumptions about the activities involved and there were many speculations about the procedures that were followed, but there were no precise details based on observations and first hand reports regarding the actual behaviour which leads to intoxication. The available literature on the subject was mainly American based and tended to present conflicting viewpoints regarding the practices. In the UK the work of Dr. Joyce Watson at Glasgow University was recognised for its value from a medical standpoint but much still remained to be classified from other angles. For example, glue sniffing practices seemed to appear suddenly in a school age population through which they would spread rapidly and then apparently disappear in the fashion of an epidemic. Similar eruptions occurred elsewhere in the community among the post school adolescent age group but despite these outbreaks there appeared to be no cohesion of knowledge on the subject. Everyone involved, it seemed, was interested solely from a particular professional angle, e.g. doctors, psychiatrists, health education officers, school, nurses, teachers, social workers, youth workers, probation officers, and others, all appeared to be working on their own without any integration of knowledge emerging from their collective experiences. Allied to this apparent scarcity of information and partly responsible for it was the widely held view, by leading members of the profession concerned, that a low profile approach to glue sniffing problems was the best policy rather than to publicise information which could possibly serve only to provoke further sniffing practices.

Public statements on glue sniffing by representatives of professional bodies tended to plead for restraint in responding to outbreaks of glue sniffing for fear of encouraging the practice further by giving undue attention to it, and also to allow time for the facts to emerge.   The principal need stated was for statistical evidence regarding the size of the problem with regard to numbers of the younger population who were at risk from the practice.   The difficulties of gathering these statistics were made worse by the previously advocated attitude of maintaining as much silence as possible on the subject.   In effect the situation current at that time was that glue sniffing cases were treated mainly with a negative response:

"There is nothing we can do for you.   You must stop this practice at once",

are common verbatim reports from sniffers who were referred for professional attention.   In extreme cases of ill health supposedly due to glue sniffing the patient was medically treated for symptoms and then discharged with warning advice.   Beyond emergency medical treatment for cases of glue sniffers who suffered physical collapse there appeared to be no organised caring response to the potentially grave health hazards risked by sniffers even when help was requested, sometimes as a matter of urgency.

After due consultations with some of my colleagues and students it was decided that the main thrust of our research investigations into solvent abuses would have to be confined towards finding effective caring responses for those who suffered ill effects from these practices.   The arduous process of collecting data on the details of glue sniffing and solvent abuse practices would have to result from actual cases who presented for treatment at the Clinic. It is important to make this direction of interest and concern clear so that the reader may appreciate that this book is first and foremost a report on the emotional aspects of glue sniffing and solvent abuse which emphasises the human interests involved.   The vital elements to which attention is focussed are the feelings of the personalities who experience solvent abuse at first hand whether it is the individual sniffer or his or her family, or friends.   A further consideration along these lines is how the members of the caring and child welfare professions feel about these practices.   The reasoning behind all this concentration on the emotional aspects of solvent abuse is the idea that the keys to understanding both why people inhale intoxicants to the extremes of chronic abuse and also to effectively helping such persons to overcome dependencies on these chemicals are the feelings they hold about themselves and other people with whom they have relationships.

Attention is directed therefore towards the emotional experiences which sniffers have in common with each other and which it is believed generate the stresses and strains which subsequently lead to intoxication practices. It is considered that subjective factors are central to appreciating the full aetiology of glue sniffing activities.

As will be shown in this book the objective findings emerging from studies of solvent abuses in the population are made credible only when they are broken down in terms of the subjective state of the individual abuser. In the final analysis it is believed that the management and treatment of behaviour problems such as solvent abuse will only be truly effective when caring approaches are aimed at the subject, the person rather than the symptomatic behaviour. The outcomes of the research studies reported in this book are believed to show how and why this is so.

2 BACKGROUND TO THE CURRENT SITUATION

When problems deriving from glue sniffing and solvent abuses by young people are considered, it is essential to view such practices in the right perspective. Although there are no known precedents for such large scale abuses by the young there is nothing new to the practice of sniffing and inhaling vapours for pleasure. While the epidemic like outbreaks affecting school children and teenagers are linked to the easy availability of modern industrial products, with the potential to seriously affect the human central nervous system, there are many antecedents to these practices. The principle on which these activities are based is a simple one. Inhaling air through the nose is a quick way of testing the environment for survival purposes. Some smells foretell danger others indicate where food and water can be found, and identify the presence of adults of the opposite sex. Yet others, mainly originating from the flowers of plants, are sheer pleasure to sniff. It is this capacity for experiencing through the sense of smell the environment in which we live which predisposes human beings to intoxication through the act of inhaling. Joyce Watson, (1982), has aptly pointed out that the large surface area of the lungs provides quick and easy access of inhalants to the body and the general effect is likely to be as rapid as that of an intravenous injection of a drug.

Evidence of the truth of the above is abundant in the recorded history of mankind. Over thousands of years people from many different cultures throughout the world have indulged activities involving the deliberate inhalation of intoxicating fumes for various purposes, mostly that of gaining inebriation.

It is interesting in an historical context to see how widespread the misuse of chemical fumes has been as a popular means of inducing states of altered consciousness. For example, there was the Pythia in ancient Greece, a young priestess, who inhaled fumes escaping through the rocks (probably carbon dioxide vapour) in order to experience visions which she would present for interpretation to the Prophet who served the Oracle at Delphi. In the Bible lands vapours from aromatic gums and burning spices were inhaled by the devout as part of the ritual of worship in Judaic culture. Further testimony to the popularity of such practices is revealed in the Biblical reference

'Ointment and perfumes rejoice the heart' (Proverbs, XXVII, 9).
Elsewhere it has been observed that behaviour involving the misuse of
drugs seems to present a recurring pattern throughout world history,
only the types of drugs abused have varied (Lewis and Patterson, 1974).
Archaeological evidence suggests that certain perfumes were liberally
used in rites of Egyptian worship while in ancient Babylon and
Palestine stone altars have been unearthed which had been used for
burning incense made from aromatic woods and spices, (Brecher, 1972).
In the New Testament there is reference to the custom of honouring
noble guests by sprinkling them with perfume and incense (St. Luke,
VII, 46).   Columbus commented upon a practice common among the West
Indian tribes he encountered of using snuff which they inhaled through
sniffing tubes, (Cohen, 1977).   Effron et al (1978) remarked upon the
popularity of tobacco, virola and other snuffs used throughout Central
and South America.   Whilst during the Renaissance, the French essayist
Montaigne noted the pleasant mindchanging effects of some odours and
wrote 'Incense and perfumes raise our spirits and excite and purify
our senses' (Essais, I, LV) a statement which was echoed much later by
his fellow countrymen Baudelaire and de Maupassant who inhaled ether
for inspiration as well as pleasure, (Preble & Laury, 1967).

Following the discovery in 1776 of nitrous oxide it was soon
realised that this gas had a stimulating and laughter producing effect
when inhaled.   In many parts of the USA there were large scale
demonstrations of laughing gas for public entertainment.

In England it became fashionable in some quarters for adults to
inhale the fumes of such substances as chloroform, ether, as well as
nitrous oxide, for leisure and recreation (Brecher, 1972).   Some
important public figures among whom were outstanding creative
personalities such as Coleridge, Southey and Wedgwood were known to
have inhaled nitrous oxide for its euphoric effects.

It is an indication of some significance that these last three
substances were abused for their intoxicating effects even before
their medical use as anaesthetics.   Cohen (1969) cites accounts of
ether and chloroform inhalation at student parties in universities at
this time in both England and the USA.   In 1855 a major outbreak of
ether sniffing occurred at Draperstown in Northern Ireland where it was
used as a substitute for alcohol following a successful temperance
movement.   Further to this there are examples drawn from other
situations where solvents have been misused as alternatives to
alcohol consumption by both men and women serving prison sentences in
the UK.   During the First World War 1914-18 there were even accounts
of allied troops sniffing fumes from the metal polish used for their
equipment.

In a contemporary vein it has been disclosed that both cocaine and
heroin can be inhaled as intoxicants and are effective if administered
intra-nasally in the same manner as snuff (Cohen, 1977).   It would
appear that 'sniffing' practices are the outcome of more profound
motivations than the simple fashionable fads they have sometimes been
thought to be, moreover they have an established history which ante-
dates modern industrial usage of solvents.

Evidence which has accumulated from studies made during the early and middle seventies has shown that solvent abuse practices are a source of serious problems among young people in many countries throughout the world. The countries which have reported such abuse to be a serious problem include the USA, Canada, Mexico and several nations of Central and South America and many European countries notably Sweden, West Germany, Hungary, Israel, Eire and the UK. From Japan there have been reports of paint thinner inhalation problems with children and adults (Sasa et al, 1978). Incidents involving the deliberate inhalation of petrol fumes have been reported among the Australian aboriginies (Nurcombe et al, 1970), the Indians of Arctic Manitoba (Boecks et al, 1976) and several countries of the African Continent (Cohen, 1977). Since the misuse of solvents for intoxication purposes has occurred so widely throughout the world spreading problems in its wake it is surprising that no concerted effort has been made by World Health Organisations to combat the spread of these practices for the sake of the health and welfare of the people involved and more especially for the protection of the young. In this latter respect it is a development of some significance that the long term abuse of chemical intoxicants such as solvents by a predominantly adolescent population represents a trend towards further proliferation in the long history of neurotoxicity.

GLUE SNIFFING AND SOLVENT ABUSE BY CHILDREN AND YOUNG ADULTS

Glue sniffing first appeared under its own heading in the Index Medicus in 1969. A great deal of the research has been done in the United States where a solvent sniffing epidemic mainly involving teenagers was first observed in the late 1950's (Bass, 1970). Two references in a pamphlet published by the Swedish Board of Health and Welfare (Stockholm, 1978) contain what appears to be the first cases to be cited in the literature of young people inhaling solvent fumes. The first refers to a fourteen year old girl who in 1900 deliberately made herself drunk by inhaling petrol fumes. The other case from the year 1937 concerned a fourteen year old schoolboy who inhaled trichloro-ethylene. In the USA the earliest published reference to glue sniffing by children was made in 1959 and concerned the wilful inhalation of glue fumes by schoolchildren in Denver, Colorado, while in Sweden cases of children sniffing paint thinner were reported from the children's village at Ska as early as 1948. Although there had been some reports of young people inhaling petrol vapour during the early 1950's it was not until 1959 that the glue and solvent sniffing craze really began in the USA.

Since then the practice by school children and adolescents has spread throughout the USA, to become a serious form of drug abuse. It was said to be occurring in every State of the USA by 1965 (Corliss, 1965) and it is thought that it subsequently arrived in the United Kingdom as an American import. Copies of a booklet entitled Glue Sniffing, Big Trouble in a Tube, by L.R. Curtis, MD, (1967) published by the General Military Training and Support Division of the US Army Department were circulating in the Strathclyde and Lanarkshire area in the early 1970's and are testimony to the American influence.

In the UK the problem first came to the attention of the authorities in the Lanarkshire area where Dr. Joyce Watson, a research fellow at Glasgow University, has pioneered the provision of caring attention for young sniffers. The statistics deriving from Scotland are sobering and give an indication of the serious nature of the problem affecting the school population. In November 1970 the abuse of solvents became official in Lanarkshire when the police encountered a group of teenagers who were acting drunk and disorderly. It later emerged that the causes of this behaviour arose from sniffing the fumes of an industrial de-greasing agent stolen locally. More incidents came to the attention of the authorities and the problem was highlighted by a particular distressing case of a ten year old boy who was discovered unconscious in a school playground suffering from the effects of inhaling shoe conditioner. In 1975 it was estimated that the number of young people in the Glasgow and surrounding areas who were participating in solvent abuse practices to be well in excess of two thousand. These statistics were compiled from information provided by social workers, police, teachers, parents and superintendents of remand homes, all of whom agreed that there are a multitude of grave social problems which are linked to the incidents of glue sniffing activities by young people. There is a significant trend to be observed in the official figures reported from Scotland which indicates that solvent abuse is affecting progressively younger age groups each year. The age range has been reported as between eight and seventeen years with an average age of twelve or thirteen years but there are alarming reports from Strathclyde and Ayrshire of glue sniffers as young as six and five years of age. Unfortunately this trend towards the abuse of solvents by even young school children is continuing and is illustrative of the critical implications the whole problem presents. Added to the problem of the escalation of glue sniffing practices in those populations where it has become established is the fact that it appears to be spreading and claiming victims elsewhere as witnessed by national and local press reports of outbreaks which appear with disturbing regularity.

The prevalence of solvent abuse throughout the UK is not very well defined but is obviously not restricted to any one geographical area. Police in the London Borough of Islington first identified glue sniffing in 1977. At the University of Newcastle upon Tyne over the one year period September 1979 to August 1980 the author received numerous enquiries requesting information on the subject from parts of the UK outside the North East region which included:

Edinburgh, Glasgow, Dunfermline, Bristol, Northamptonshire, Lancashire, Exeter, London, Romford, Wolverhampton and Co. Antrim, Northern Ireland, (see figure 1.2.)

At the Poisons Unit in Guys Hospital, London, the requests received for information during the year July 1980 to June 1981 concerned 324 patients (226 male, 98 female) whose ages ranged from 3 to 31 years who were suspected of solvent abuse (Francis et al, 1982).

14

The National Health Service Regions involved in these requests comprised the following:

Northern, Trent, The Thames Areas, West Midlands, Mersey, Yorkshire, East Anglia, Wessex, Oxford, South Western, North Western.

Gay and his team of investigators (1982) surveyed a large urban area in the County of Avon and received 413 incidents of abuse involving 304 young persons during six months. Again in the North Eastern Region of Newcastle upon Tyne the author researched the Police referrals of solvent abuse to Social Services during the period January to December 1982 and the results can be seen in figure 2.1. Although these figures cannot be interpreted as indicating total prevalence since many cases would be undetected they are nonetheless a firm estimate of the size of the problem which necessitates immediate attention.

A disturbing feature of these statistics on Police referrals has latterly begun to emerge. It appears that the incidents of glue sniffing and solvent abuse reported by the Police are beginning to decrease in number which might apparently indicate a recession in the activities of abuse throughout the region. Careful enquiry into this development has revealed however that the fall in figures is more likely to be due to the fact that police officers are not reporting the incidents of solvent abuse which they encounter since it would appear that such referrals rarely lead to any effective response from the social services. It seems overall that glue sniffing and solvent abuses by the young are a cause for embarrassment generally to the child welfare and caring services who on the whole are unable to respond with any effective strategies. It is ominous that such apathy can lead to acceptance which is what appears to be happening since it is a matter of observation that young people can be seen sniffing openly in public places.

It is interesting to reflect that ethyl alcohol or ethanol when it was first used to stupify, around 2,000 BC was a secret and guarded practice reserved for special occasions and rituals of celebration. With open usage came social acceptance and it has taken thousands of years for us to recognise the potential for disease that alcohol abuses can initiate. The evidence is already beginning to accumulate that solvent abuses once limited to a young teenage culture with an average age of 14 to 15 years are becoming popular with age groups in the early and middle twenties. Undoubtedly in these times of economic hardship for many these intoxicants are easily available and are attractively priced in comparison with alcohol. Yet another important consideration is that they have a faster intoxicating action than alcohol and tend to be more potent in the inebriating effects they cause.

1982 SOLVENT ABUSE REFERRALS - DIVISIONAL/MONTHLY BREAKDOWN

	Total	Boys	Girls	A	B	C	D	E	F
January	35	24	11	2	19	6	4	4	0
February	87	71	16	6	23	13	23	12	10
March	104	87	17	5	40	25	17	7	10
April	59	50	9	1	24	8	6	19	1
May	62	42	20	4	32	11	6	6	3
June	28	28	0	1	19	1	4	3	0
July	41	31	10	8	17	8	4	0	4
August	51	41	10	10	18	5	9	5	4
September	48	43	5	11	20	1	9	6	1
October	41	35	6	11	15	4	3	5	3
November	29	22	7	3	10	5	7	3	1
December	42	36	6	3	11	12	3	2	11
	627	510	117	65	248	99	95	72	48

Percentage of boys = 81%

Percentage of girls = 19%

Age range: 12 to 17 years

Average age: boys - 15 years

Average age: girls - 14 years

Highest concentration of sniffers according to above referrals = city centre area.

Only small numbers in country areas = area A. (see map)

Peak period of year for referrals: February, March, April.

N.B. A cautionary note is essential here to emphasise that police patrols are more active in city than country areas.

Figure 2.1

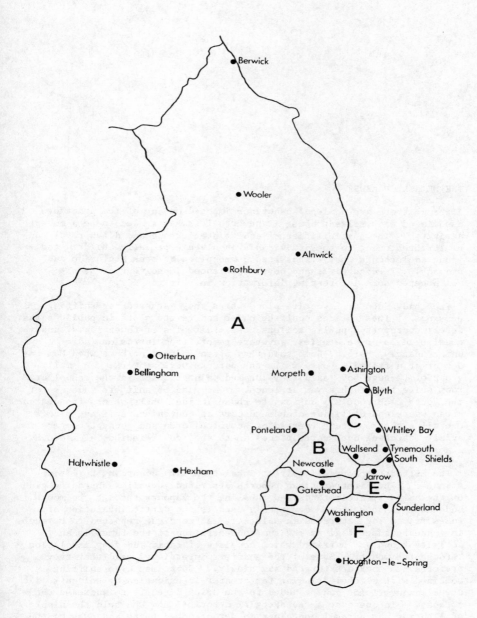

THE METHOD OF ABUSE

Although there are no legal sanctions imposed on any of the practices
associated with solvent abuse it nevertheless has tended to be a covert
activity.   The possibilities of adult interference and disapproval can
be so threatening to the individuals involved especially children and
young adolescents that it has been commonplace to seek seclusion and
privacy.   Teenage girls and boys experienced in solvent abuse
volunteered some interesting information in this respect.

   They had a den or favourite place where they gathered for sniffing
sessions.   These places could be quiet and remote spots in public parks,
derelict property, public toilets, the stairwells of tower flats, under
canal bridges or cemeteries, anywhere remote from intrusion and,
unfortunately, help.   Some said they often sniffed at home when Mum was
out or at a friend's house while the parents were at work.   A small
group of teenage boys said they inhaled paint thinner in the school art
room while the teacher was at lunch.   One gang of sniffers made use of
the youth club roof all unknown to those inside, while others frequented
urban wasteland utilising abandoned cars as convenient sniffing places.
Overall a clear picture emerged of schoolchildren and young teenagers
avidly searching out secret places where they could imbibe intoxicating
fumes.

   The methods employed in solvent inhalation vary according to circumstances.   The first American reports described juveniles spreading glue
on the palms of their hands and inhaling the vapours through the mouth
and nose.   Another method commonly used is the direct inhalation of
fumes from a rag saturated in solvent.   A technique reported to be much
in vogue because it gives maximum concentration of the fumes is an
activity known as 'huffing' which consists of rapid and deep inhalation
through the mouth.   Some of the sniffers interviewed said that they
preferred to suck a saturated rag slowly.   Sometimes glue sniffing is
combined with alcohol drinking for greater intoxication or solvents like
dry-cleaning fluids can be added to the drink directly to increase the
potency.   In one case a teenage girl described how she held the nipple
of a butane gas aerosol container in her clenched teeth and pressed the
can to spray directly into her mouth.   One group of teenage boys and
girls said they poured dry-cleaning fluid onto the sleeves and lapels

18

of their coats and sniffed from there.   In the case of adhesives the specific method of choice usually involved the use of a small polythene or plastic bag, in early cases a small potato crisp bag with a capacity of 500 ml was favoured.   The glue was squeezed from a tube or poured from a tin into the bag to a depth of approximately 1 inch at the bottom.   The open end of the bag was then placed over the mouth and nose.   Deep breathing for 12 to 20 breaths would then take place until the desired state of intoxication was achieved.   This method involved rebreathing and sometimes large polythene bags were placed over the head and neck to trap the fumes and enhance the intoxication.   Tins of glue could also be heated to accelerate the emission of fumes.   The technique of rebreathing repeatedly from a plastic bag tends to incur the additional health hazards of hypoxia (oxygen deficiency) and hypercarbia (abnormally high concentrations of carbon dioxide in the blood).

Dry cleaning substance vapours were inhaled directly from the tops of bottles or alternatively from rags or handkerchiefs saturated with the fluid and then placed as a pad over the nose or mouth.   Nail polish remover was used in the same way.

One reported method of gaining access to intoxicating fumes was for a group of sniffers to tour new developments on housing estates searching for skips containing large used containers of adhesive which still contained enough resin to give off strong vapours when heated. Needless to say the fire risk of this practice is considerable and has resulted in many injuries as well as damage to property.

Any kind of container that is readily to hand will do and it is not unusual to find milk bottles, soft drink bottles, empty jam jars, tins and coffee jars pressed into service as receptacles for solvents.   Many of those interviewed stressed that it was safest to sniff in a group so that others could help if anything went wrong.   They meant the sort of tragedies which periodically appear in the press reporting that another teenager has been found dead after a lone sniffing session during which he collapsed unconscious and was suffocated by the plastic bag over his head or while unconscious he vomited and choked to death.

As an alternative to or in addition to glue sniffing, many teenagers inhale the hydro-carbons and solvents to be found in aerosols.   There have been alarming reports of aerosols sprayed directly into the nose or mouth but usually the substance is sprayed into a plastic or paper bag and inhaled from there.

THE PRODUCTS ABUSED

It seems that the use of any particular agent for purposes of inhalation is related to such factors as availability, cost and accessibility.   It is a cause of serious reflection and possibly some alarm when it is realised that most of the products listed in the chart on p 3   can be freely purchased cheaply by the youngest children.   They can all be easily stolen, and often are, if not from supermarkets and the like, they can be taken without any bother from ordinary household kitchens, workshops and garages.   Many of the products listed like hair-spray

and plastic cement for model making are often given to children and
teenagers as presents.   While in schools it is not hard to find easy
access to paints, thinners and glues for the enterprising sniffer.
The chart on p.3 gives an indication of the range of products which
are commonly abused and it is clear from this that products containing
Toluene, like glues, plastic cements and paint thinners, are most
popular.   But in cases of habitual sniffing it would seem that any
product containing volatile substances will do and some bizarre
examples are on record: drinking paraffin oil and sniffing a steradent
tablet shoved up the nose; drinking the chlorinated water in public
swimming baths: inhaling household bleach and sniffing 'fire
extinguishers'. Such an extensive range of products liable to abuse
has prompted successive government ministers at the Department of
Health and Social Security (DHSS) to comment that it was not
practicable to impose controls over all the products which could give
'kicks to sniffers'.   Further to this it is necessary to emphasise
that the variety of products abused does present a dangerous possibility
that sniffers will learn to experiment.   Some studies from the USA
appear to indicate that young people with a history of solvent sniffing
are much more likely to become addicted to hard drugs in later life as
if, it seems, they are predisposed by habit to search for stronger and
stronger drugs to satisfy their developing needs for pleasure and
escape, (D'Amanda et al, 1977).

PATTERNS OF USE

Glue sniffing and solvent abuse practices are indulged principally by
young people and by a minority of the very young.   A study reported
by 1974 by the Institute for the Study of Drug Dependence (ISDD)
entitled The Deliberate Inhalation of Volatile Substances states that
the overwhelming majority of those who inhale solvent vapours and
aerosol sprays are aged between 10 and 15 years, and mentions further
that a significant minority of youths under the age of 10 years are
known to indulge the practice.

 A study reported by Watson (1982) of the solvent abuse cases
referred to her over the six year period 1975 to 1981 revealed that the
age range was considerably wider in the west of Scotland as compared
with the population in the ISDD study referred to above.   In Watson's
sample the ages were from 8 to 19 years, although it was indicated
that the majority of sniffers were in the young teenage group of
between 13 to 15 years.   It is interesting to reflect that the
statistics relating to numbers of sniffers within the population
appear to derive solely from cases in which a crisis has occurred
necessitating intervention by the police or members of the caring
professions.

 Reports on the frequency of involvement tend to vary.   It would seem
that while many young people dabble in solvent abuses for some it
becomes a regular habit.   Watson refers to 40 cases from her sample
who were involved on a daily basis some for almost every day for
eighteen months or more with an amount of substance which varied from
a tube of glue which lasted weeks to a daily consumption of 3-4
pints of glue.

With regard to the kind of person who inhales solvents it is interesting to note that studies in the USA of typologies of glue and volatile substance sniffing are born out by indications from research at the University of Newcastle upon Tyne. A review of the American surveys (Stash, 1974) reports findings which distinguish between two classes of sniffers. The first is a general population who are experimenting with glue sniffing. Young people, mainly teenagers of school age copy sniffing activities of their peer group to be in fashion. It is a novel and new experience which can heighten feelings of belonging within adolescent subcultures. For example, sniffers attending the University Counselling Clinic often reported first contacts with solvents abuse in friendship groups formed at Comprehensive School. Interviews with sniffers who professed membership of rival teenage groups in the North Eastern region revealed that being a member of a punk or skinhead group was sometimes conditional upon joining sniffing parties. A 15 year old girl reported joining a punk group who had forced entry into some boarded up derelict property. The following extract from her account gives a vivid description of the scene she experienced:

'Some of the group were living there. A few were on the run from Homes* others were wanted by the Police. The boys had fixed up lights and cassette recorders to run off batteries they had stolen from cars. There was nothing to eat but there was stacks of glue. Tracey and me saw a cupboard filled with tins of glue and thinners which had been stolen. There was this green bucket with a towel over it. It had glue, thinners, petrol, cleaners and some other things all mixed up and it was passed around. If you wanted to stay you had to put the towel over your head and breathe in from the bucket. We kept passing out and coming round and sniffing again all day and night. Then the police raided us and we got caught.'

In contrast to those who only dabble in sniffing activities are the young people who adopt a habitual pattern of inhaling volatile fumes often for an appreciable amount of time each day. Such cases are diagnosed as chronic and display an obvious need to sniff regularly as a dependent pattern of behaviour. The development of dependency on the inhalation of volatile fumes will be discussed in the following section under effects. Here it is sufficient to say that not all sniffers develop dependencies on solvents. It seems that for many young people sniffing practices are a kind of teenage dare, a way of responding to the challenge of authority. But a minority find that the practice is tension reducing and a pleasant escape from a boring and frustrating world. These sniffers have problems with which they cannot normally cope. For them sniffing becomes a vital source of relief from everyday worries and their behaviour tends to become more and more a withdrawal into a phantasy world away from all the cares of family, school and peer group relationships. While it is true that only a limited number of sniffers become chronically involved nevertheless every chronic sniffer was at one time a dabbler.

* Residential Care establishments.

The danger is that adverse environmental conditions added to the stresses and strains of maturation during adolescence may increase the numbers of young people who become vulnerable to the attractions of solvent intoxication. Further to this is the risk that inhalation abuses by the young may become socially accepted due to public and professional apathy in regard to the problem.

The patterns of glue sniffing and solvent abuse are already apparent in the behaviour of many young people especially those who live in the highly populated areas of cities throughout the UK. The signs are that these practices have the potential to rank alongside alcohol and drug abuse as primary generators of serious problems which require caring interventions. Not least of all in respect of the intoxicating effects.

3 THE EFFECTS

It is difficult to understand why young people deliberately inhale solvent fumes to extreme states of intoxication especially when the effects are considered.   But just as the hangover effects of alcohol in no way ensures that the sufferer will cease to drink too much again so the habitual sniffer is apparently able to withstand many ill effects as the inevitable outcomes of solvent abuse without necessarily ever wanting to stop the practice.   When it is realised that some unfortunate cases sniff themselves to death the nature of the powerful hold that solvent abuse can develop over the person is appreciated. In figure 3.1 can be seen the list of presenting symptoms of glue sniffing and solvent abuse which have been listed in treatment sessions at the Counselling Clinic in the University of Newcastle upon Tyne. These symptoms, which alone are serious enough to warrant a treatment response, represent only one aspect of the suffering which the inhalation of toxic vapours can cause for the individual.

   In comparison with other misbehaviours which society deplores in the young such as excessive alcohol consumption, habitual cigarette smoking and sexual delinquency, solvent abuse ranks alongside the misuse of drugs as potentially most damaging.   Dr. Joyce Watson, as a result of long experience with sniffers, comments on the special hazards involved:

    'It disturbs me that a child can have an accident the first
    time he tries.   I have known children who sniffed glue once
    and died.' (Kerr, 1979).

This latter quotation raises what is the most frightening effect of all to contemplate, the possibility of fatalities among solvent abusers. Although the numbers of those who die from sniffing are relatively small in comparison with road deaths it is disturbing to reflect that it is the young and healthy who are being killed through self induced poisoning.   Further analysis of the fatalities from sniffing reveal many significant features.

LIST OF PRESENTING CLINICAL
SYMPTOMS OF SOLVENT ABUSERS

Headaches, sometimes lasting for days.
Sore eyes
Nasal discharge,
Sore throat
Chest pains
Heart palpitations
Shortness of breath
Stomach cramps
Pain in side - stitch pains
Aching legs - especially calves
Sharp pains in either or both sides of lower back
Pain when urinating
Constipation and diarrhoea
Vomiting and feeling nausea
Numbness in extremities, e.g. toes, fingers,
Numbness in cheek
Dental pains and discomforts
Sweating
Hand tremors and body shakes
Insomnia
Feelings of ground moving
Confusion
Feelings of not really being here, i.e. watching oneself
Convulsions
Feelings of persecution
Paranoia
Feelings of being touched by unseen hands, animals, insects
Pain behind the eyes
Hallucinations of various forms
Dialogues with God and Devil
Hearing voices
Imagining feelings of impossible power, e.g. ability to fly, feats of
    strength associated with comic strip heroes
Possession by evil entities
Dream states
Walking and running difficulties
Unable to focus and double vision
Smelling substances in their absence
Heightened sensitivity to noise
Feelings of muscles somewhere in the body going into spasm
Feelings of lightness and alternatively heaviness
Suicidal thoughts
Self mutilation thoughts
Feelings of hyperactivity
Feelings of not wanting to associate with people, of wanting to hide
Sensations of being pricked as with needles in different parts of
    the body
Depression and anxiety
Feelings of being afraid without apparent cause

Figure 3.1

DEATHS

In respect of the deaths which occur as a result of inhaling chemical fumes it is important to distinguish between cases in which the causes of death appear to be only indirectly associated with the abuse of solvent fumes or vapours from a volatile substance and those which occur due to the direct toxic effects of the substance inhaled. Examples of the former are deaths resulting from accidental injury inflicted whilst intoxicated, suffocation where a plastic bag was found over the person's head or covering the vital nose and mouth air passageways, and asphyxia due to inhalation of stomach contents occurring when the person vomitted while collapsed. With regards to deaths caused by the direct toxic effects of the chemical fumes on the functioning of essential body organs it is worth noting that aerosol sprays are possibly the most dangerous. There have been reports of aerosol spraying directly into the nose or mouth which can cause instant death (Watson, 1976).

It cannot be overstressed that inhaling the sprays of certain aerosols which contain volatile hydro-carbons (see list on chart pp 3 and 4 is life threatening even when inhaled indirectly from a bag. The danger of this malpractice is that it can cause death instantaneously. An epidemic of a hundred and ten sudden deaths occurred among American youths during the 1960's. These deaths were not due to plastic bag suffocation but appear to have been the immediate result of inhaling volatile hydrocarbons like trichlorethane and fluorinated refrigerants. The poisonous effects seem to have been intensified by stress or activity of some kind. It appears that in these American cases the heart just stopped beating, causing instant death. The story of how this research survey emerged is hardly surprising in view of the subsequent findings. Simply by chance a sudden death in a solvent sniffer came to the attention of Dr. Millard Bass, a forensic pathologist. A survey by telephone of medical examiners' offices confirmed his suspicions that similar cases of sudden sniffing deaths were occurring elsewhere. A nationwide survey in 1969 left no doubt that there was an epidemic. A significant feature of the investigations into these sudden deaths is the mystery surrounding the precise reason for the fatality. Autopsies on the victims, whose ages ranged from eleven to twenty three years, revealed no anatomical cause of death. A further disturbing factor in all these cases emerged, it seems that there was some kind of stressful activity or reaction which closely accompanied the inhalation of the poisonous chemicals and which appears to be related to the sudden death. It is a sobering thought that similar tragedies may be happening in other places and escape detection due to the lack of knowledge on this crucial issue.

Further to the above it would appear that the whole question of how potentially lethal are the volatile substances abused by sniffers has been clouded by the over zealous supporters of the low profile approach to the problem. The way in which the numbers of deaths occurring through volatile substance abuses can fail to be monitored through lack of mention of the substances on some death certificates is highlighted in a study by Anderson et al (1982). Over the period 1971 to 1981 a total of 169 deaths associated with volatile substance abuse in the UK were recorded. A number of points emerging from this study deserve special mention here.   Briefly they are:

During 1981 the deaths from Volatile Substance Abuse (VSA)
numbered 45.   VSA deaths appeared to account for over 1%
of deaths from all causes and nearly 2% of deaths from
injury and poisoning in males between the ages of 10 and
19 years.

The chief substances involved were butane, solvents in
adhesives, e.g. Toluene, other solvents such as trichloro
ethane and carbon tetrochloride, fire extinguisher substance
bromochlorofluoromethane (BCF).

It was observed that solvents in adhesives became more
important with increasing age.

The deaths occurred in most cases while the person was alone
at home.   In approximately 40% of cases death appeared to be
only indirectly associated with VSA since it involved injury
through accident, or plastic bag over head or choking because
of inhalation of stomach contents.   Nearly half of the
deaths were attributed to the direct toxic effects of the
substance inhaled, the proportion was highest with aerosols
and lowest with solvents in adhesives although it was
recognised that toluene inhalation carries less risk of
sudden death nevertheless it is clear that sudden death can
occur following the inhalation of toluene, e.g. glue fumes.

The statistics relating to deaths among adolescents resulting either
directly or indirectly from the deliberate inhalation of fumes from
volatile substances are grave enough in themselves to warrant action
to stop the practice spreading and claiming further victims.   But the
individual case histories of fatalities make sombre reading.   It is
surely impossible for a caring adult to accept that a young person
should not be protected by the full power of the law and the conscience
of society against death by self poisoning occurring through the
misguided pursuit of pleasure.   The following case is typical of many
deaths only certain details have been changed.

Roy, a 16 year old was watching TV with his elder brother on a
Saturday afternoon in the Autumn of 1980.   His brother went
into the kitchen leaving Roy relaxing in an armchair by the
fire.   Returning to the lounge some minutes later he saw that
Roy was standing near the fireplace swaying from side to side.
There was a yellow coloured cloth in his right hand and an
aerosol spray can in his left.   He was dribbling at the mouth
and slavering down the front of his clothes.   His brother
yelled at him to stop and ran over to take the materials away
from him.   He managed to grab the can but Roy kept putting
the rag to his mouth and nose.   After a brief struggle Roy
pushed his brother over and ran to the window and as he did
so he began gasping for air.   He could not open the window.
He then ran past his brother through the kitchen and out the
back door.   He was running very fast as he went through the
garden and up the hill.   His brother was running after him
but Roy ran much faster.   He got nearly to the top of the

26

hill when his brother saw him stagger and fall face downwards.
An eye witness said: 'We caught up with Roy as he collapsed
and saw that his mouth was wide open, his lips a blue colour,
the tongue was white and his eyes were half closed. Spittle
was bubbling from his mouth, all the time we watched him.
Soon an ambulance came and took him away'.

Roy was found to be dead on admission to the local General
Hospital.   The forensic post mortem report stated that the
cause of death was due to (or as a consequence of) cardio
respiratory failure and inhalation of Pain Relieving Spray
(fluorohydrocarbons).

In figure 3.2 there are listed some other examples of deaths linked to
volatile substance abuse which illustrate the variety of everyday
products which have a lethal potential and the different circumstances
in which death has occurred.   In each case where a young person has
died from sniffing activities there is the consequent aftermath of
sorrow and recriminations.   There are the bereaved relatives to
consider.   Lives ruined by the loss of a son or daughter.   Guilt
feelings generated by the inevitable thought that the death was
unnecessary and could perhaps have been avoided.   Meanwhile the deaths
continue to occur raising implications quite beyond the mortalities to
the question of possible long term health hazards risked by the chronic
sniffers who survive.

The effects of solvent abuse appear to be subject to variation
according to individual factors such as: age, physique, personality,
type and length of sniffing history and the amount of a particular
substance inhaled (Wyse, 1973).   These effects may vary from an acute
state of inebriation resembling alcoholic intoxication to behaviour
disorders and the experience of abnormal mental states.   Psychiatric
and psychological sources suggest that the prior emotional and physical
experience of the user may significantly influence the effects (Lewis
and Patterson, 1974).   From a summary of the effects of solvent abuse
it can be seen that initially, at the experiential level the effects
seem to be mild excitement and euphoria.   Users spoke of a 'buzzing
noise' which left them dizzy and confused.

A 14 year old girl glue sniffer's comments are typical of many when
describing the attractions of the intoxicating effects:

'It felt marvellous and stupendous.   There was this feeling
of floating and having no weight you know as if you were
really free of everything and could go where you like.
There was nothing to worry about because you couldn't
remember.   Most of the time you felt grand and you could
feel yourself laughing and really having fun and a good
time.   Everybody was nice to each other and said really
funny things.   It was great.   Then you get illusions and
they are wonderful and you don't want them to stop.   That's
why I sniff'.

A more objective description of the immediate effects of intoxication
through sniffing is indicated by Watson (1977).   Self control and the
will to direct behaviour is rapidly lost at this stage and similarly

27

Figure 3.2

ADOLESCENT DEATHS LINKED TO VOLATILE ABUSE FROM PRESS REPORTS

SEX AND AGE	PLACE OF DEATH	VOLATILE SUBSTANCE INHALED	PRESS SOURCE	DATE AND CAUSE OF DEATH
Boy 16 yrs.	Killa Marsh, Sheffield	Liquid Lighter Fuel, Kerosene	Sheffield Star, 14.5.80	April — Coma and dead on admission to Hallam-shire Hpl. Sheffield.
Boy 16 yrs.	Police Cells, Vine St. London	Glue containing Toluene	Evening Standard 15.2.80	1.2.80 — Found collapsed with other prisoner on top of him in cell. Police surgeon pronounced him dead.
Girl 15 yrs.	Front room of house	Butane gas aerosol	Daily Telegraph 12.8.80	10.8.80 — Coroner's verdict accidental death. Pathologist stated death caused by toxic and anaesthetic effects on lungs and heart of inhaled butane gas.
Girl 16 yrs.	Collapsed dying on dance floor at disco in Bourne-mouth	Cleaning fluid Trichlorethane	Daily Mirror 31.7.80	27.5.80 — Pathologist stated death due to inhaling chemical fumes in cleaning fluid.
Boy 14 yrs.	Stobhill Hpl. Glasgow	Fluid from fire extinguisher stolen from British Rail.	Glasgow Herals 19.5.80	27.5.80 — Coma and death in hospital

The above examples are taken from a total of 29 known deaths assoc. with VSA in Uk. (Ref. Anderson et al, 1982)

muscular co-ordination and orientation. Delusions of perception gradually give way to hallucinations followed by stupor and unconsciousness.

When considering the effects from a broader viewpoint it becomes clear that the inhalation of volatile substances affects the individual in a multitude of ways. It would be a mistake to consider only the physical effects as if sniffing practices posed only medical problems. A close study of the activities overall reveals that the ill effects on both the social and personal life of the individual are every bit as critical. It is essential therefore to discuss the effects under three main headings which are the physical, the social and the psychological effects.

THE PHYSICAL EFFECTS

Observation and examination of cases attending the University Counselling Clinic already mentioned produced a typical pattern of signs at the physical and behavioural level which are summarised briefly here:

Physical Signs   A blank dreamy look. Enlarged pupils. Red spots and marks around mouth and nose. Strong smell of solvents about the person, on the breath, on hair, on clothing. Self-inflicted tattoos, self mutilations.   Glue stains on clothing, bed clothes, window sills, door handles, carpeting, towels, tissues, etc. Signs such as bottles or plastic bags containing hardened glue, empty aerosol tins.

Personal Signs   A dreamy, drowsy look. Lack of concentration. Loss of appetite, drunken behaviour, listless, moody, and easily annoyed. Unexplained fits of temper, inability to remember things that have recently happened and a tendency to isolation.   A change in normal habits, staying out later, not attending school.   Acting suspiciously and out of character. (O'Connor, 1981).

Volatile substances can have a serious poisoning effect on the body when inhaled in concentrated form over a lengthy period of time.   The symptoms of intoxication naturally vary with the strength and type of substance abused but figure   gives some indications of the effects of intoxication which have been reported by sniffers.   At their most vivid the experiences affecting the central nervous system (CNS) are such that the brain begins to malfunction and the sensory information such as vision, hearing, touch, smell, taste and movement which is fed to the brain becomes distorted.   These effects are the result of the drugs which have been absorbed quickly as vapours through the lung tissues and then via the bloodstream to the brain.   Illusions, dreams, hallucinations and nightmares are commonly experienced by sniffers at this stage and are for the most part desired effects.   Habitual sniffing can also lead to the emergence of observable effects which may easily identify the sniffer.   Some of these effects are listed in figure 3.3.

VOLATILE SUBSTANCE ABUSE (VSA)

Some of the observable intoxicating effects on the appearance
and behaviour of sniffers and possible identifying signs

Facial Blemishes, spots and sores especially around the mouth and nose, cracked lips, pallid, tired look, enlarged pupils, bloodshot eyes. Hair, skin, clothing and personal possessions may be stained and smell of Glue. Breath will smell of solvents. Drop in personal standards of hygiene. Immediately following inhalation may look flushed and excited, show trembling of limbs. The person can temporarily lose consciousness. Users suffer:
sore eyes, nose bleeds, sore throat, headaches, nausea, various body pains and hallucinations, pallor, torpor, unexplained fatigue, excessive thirst, loss of appetite, rapid weight loss, forgetfulness.
Signs such as:
freezer bags, milk bottles, crisp packets, plastic bread bags containing hardened glues left lying around. Stains on clothing bed clothes, window ledges, carpets. Light stains caused by excessive use of dry cleaning fluids on sleeves or lapels of clothing.
Empty containers:
Tubes, tins, bottles and aerosol cans may draw attention to 'sniffers'.

The effects of VSA Intoxication follow rapidly the inhalation, normally within minutes. Similar behaviour to alcohol intoxication. Responses of individual will vary according to personality, age, body size, weight, the type and amount of solvent inhaled. Two broad patterns of response to intoxication by volatiles, which may feature successively in the behaviour.
1. Excitatory
Loud, excited, aggressive, hostile, violent and destructive, hyperactivity, moody, easily annoyed. In extreme cases the individual may suffer seizures and convulsions.
2. Depressant
Sleepy, relaxed, failure to concentrate, marked lack of attention, yawning and apparent drowsiness, dizzy, confused, staggering, peculiar gait, talking to self in dream state, slurred speech.
General
Decline in school performance. Will lose all interest in attending school. Will tend to steal solvents or money to finance the abuse. As dependency on solvents grows the individual will tend to become more secretive, isolated from family and normal community and will tend to opt out of recreational activities.

figure 3.3

The ill effects of inhaling volatile substances achieve the most meaningful recognition when they present as identifiable changes in the individual's appearance, behaviour and awareness. For example the case of David highlights the ill effects which can disable the person:

> David is 17 years old, he has been inhaling glue and solvent fumes for well over two years and has developed a strong dependency. His tolerance level for glue solvent has risen over the period of his sniffing and he requires approximately ½ litre a day to feel right. When he first attended the University Counselling Clinic he reported the following symptoms:

> > Stomach ache and cramps. Feelings of being depressed. Stinging sensation in the eyes and ringing sounds in the head. Inability to remember what happened. Back pains in both flanks above the buttocks. Needing to use the toilet more frequently to urinate and sometimes passing blood in both urine and excrement. Soreness around the elbows and knee joints. Tingling sensations on the skin areas of arms and legs making him want to scratch a lot. Sharp headaches localised in the forehead areas if he tries to read and dull aches in the back of the head when he closes his eyes. On one occasion he recalls that he was sniffing with friends and he collapsed, and suffered what seemed to be an epileptic fit. He can just recall his friends holding him as he vomitted on the ground after the seizure.

BODY DAMAGE EFFECTS

During the course of an intense and prolonged sniffing session there are high concentrations of poisonous substances which are circulated through the body in the bloodstream. This may lead to lasting damage to the Central Nervous System and the brain, the heart, liver and the kidneys and may damage the vital blood producing function of the bone marrow. Information compiled in a most valuable little pamphlet by Scholtes & Senior (1983) summarises the injurious outcomes that can result from prolonged exposure to volatile substance fumes. In chronic cases of sniffing the major organs of the body are affected and begin to malfunction leading to serious health risks for the individual. Kidney problems are realised when protein and blood begin to appear in urine following sniffing sessions. In the interviews recorded at the University Counselling Clinic some young people have actually complained that sniffing can cause difficulties in urinating with consequent pain and alarm as in the case of David cited previously. The hard evidence on toxic effects to the kidneys is more difficult to find. Black (1982) refers to findings of renal damage ranging from transcient RBC's and proteinuria to apparently reversible renal shutdown reported by Will and McLaren (1981). A paper by Kroeger et al (1980) pointed to the life threatening effects on the kidneys of toluene inhalation.

Smith, (1976) points out that there is good reason to suspect that petrol sniffing (benzene) and aerosol abuse (halogenated hydrocarbons) can be harmful to kidneys and liver. These indications are enough to warrant serious attention.

With regard to brain damage caused by sniffing there is an abundance of anecdotal evidence from clinical case reports but not much empirically acceptable evidence from a scientific viewpoint. In this respect it is essential to discriminate between two attitudes to Volatile Substance Abuse which are not necessarily opposed but which represent different viewpoints and aims. On the one hand there is the objectively oriented social science approach to problems of this kind which favours survey type investigations of population showing normal distribution characteristics and which produce valid and reliable statistical analyses. In sharp contrast is the approach incumbent upon the clinical therapist who is working in depth and over a lengthy period of time with a small group of patients who present a mass of subjective data which has undoubted reality within the therapeutic relationship. Preferably the two methods of approaching the problem should be complementary but in fact they often tend to be antithetical. For example, the counsellor caring for a sniffer who presents symptoms such as:

severe headaches, eye pains, dental pains, slurred speech, limb spasms and tremors, nausea and vomitting, amnesia and inability to concentrate, hallucinations, feelings of being two persons in the same body, lack of co-ordination,

has of necessity to work with the reality of what the patient presents which are in this case indications of mental disturbance and impairment of the brain functioning grave enough to justify immediate caring interventions. Whether this conclusion meets with the academic niceties of conclusive type evidence is irrelevant at that time to the suffering of the sniffer and the demand for the skills of the therapist. A pragmatic approach is favoured which attempts to care in the best possible way for the sniffer who is presenting needs and problems. Here it is being suggested that caring practice and theoretical analysis should ideally proceed together with the welfare of young people in mind. The findings of the following studies are presented as being significant in the light of what has been written above.

Towfighi et al (1976) concluded on the basis of intensive medical analysis in two case studies of prolonged glue sniffing, both men of 19 and 22 years respectively, that extreme sensorimotor damage was the outcome of n-hexane inhalation. Eric and Betsy Comstock (1977) summarised the clinical syndromes of selected cases from the literature and some of their findings seem to indicate the development of heart, kidney and liver diseases in addition to brain damage resulting from high concentrations of solvents in the body system. Further case study analyses of a 14 year old boy and a girl of 15, both suffering from organic lead poisoning due to habitual petrol sniffing, revealed damage to the major organs of the body and the central nervous system (CNS) (Robinson, 1978). From a summary of clinical and laboratory investigations in 132 cases of solvent abuse Watson (1978) was able to point out that, although there was an apparent absence of chronic damage in these cases, it was desirable to have long term follow ups

32

since the toxic effects may not be noticeable for many years (c.f...
alcohol), even when the concentrations of solvents achieved were low.
From the University of Kyoto in Japan, Sasa et al report finding atrophy
of the mid brain and cerebrum. Degeneration of the cerebellum was also
suspected in this case of a Japanese male aged 27 years who became
habituated to sniffing glue and thinners after 17 years of age. The
authors noted the similarities of long term toluene inhalation in their
patient and a report by Grabski in 1961, which was confirmed by Knox and
Nelson, (1966), working with the same patient, who discovered clinical
evidence linking what appeared to be irreversible brain damage with
toluene sniffing.

   In the same vein a study by Mary King (1982) of the effects of Toluene
on the CNS has raised some controversy. King states that her evidence
shows conclusively that toluene may lead to permanent neurological
damage but there has been some criticism that the design of her study
did not permit conclusive implications to be drawn. Further to this
Ashton*(1983) comments that although other evidence does suggest a link
between brain damage and extensive inhalation of toluene, as for example
in regular glue sniffing, solvent abuse of this duration and intensity
is very atypical behaviour indeed. Unfortunately, this latter statement does not appear to take account of a trend towards sniffing
practices involving progressively younger age groups already noted
elsewhere. Also there are indications that glue sniffing activities
are being continued by young people beyond the mid teens and into early
twenties, by a trickle of recent cases noted at the University
Counselling Clinic. A case reference in respect of the latter will
illustrate some of the contemporary trends among long term sniffers
which could possibly lead to the practice becoming more widespread.

   Joanne is 19 years old with a three month old son to Michael
   23 years old and unemployed with whom she has lived for the
   last two years. At one time they sniffed together but she
   stopped when she became pregnant in case the baby would be
   harmed. Michael has continued to inhale glue fumes and
   latterly his behaviour has become so bizarre that Joanne is
   afraid for their baby. Since Michael tends to sniff mainly
   at night Joanne has taken to lying awake to prevent him harming
   the baby whilst intoxicated. Recently matters came to a head
   when Joanne awoke late one night to find the baby and Michael
   gone. She found them both naked in the garden her intoxicated
   husband talking to the shivering baby showing him the moon.
   Michael says that he prefers glue sniffing to drinking alcohol
   even if he could afford the latter which he cannot since he
   became unemployed. He added that when he is high on glue he
   doesn't know what is happening and he is also scared that he
   might harm the baby. He complained of ill health due to glue
   sniffing which he insisted he is powerless to stop.

   As this case highlights it is possible that for some young people
economic hardship together with out of work frustration and boredom
could well lead to volatile substance abuses claiming habitués in the
adult population. Finally it would appear that of all the effects of
sniffing dangerous chemicals the physical effects tend to earn the most
attention. Many of these effects as already mentioned demand medical
attention and treatment often to save lives and relieve painful

conditions but it would be an error to regard the misuse of volatiles only as a medical problem in view of the multitude of ill effects which are revealed only in a social context and which require responses which are no less caring but which are family and community based.

THE SOCIAL ILL EFFECTS

By far the most damaging effect of sniffing volatiles on the life of the person is the way in which normal relationships are disrupted and the potential for such relationship impaired.   It has long been recognised with reference to alcohol drunkeness that the behaviour of the person can deteriorate to socially unacceptable levels.   A broadly similar set of effects is noted with regard to adolescent behaviour when young people are inebriated by solvents and other volatiles.

   Initially there is an observable weakening of behaviour controls with a subsequent lowering of standards which become intolerable to non sniffers in the family or group.   Tempers flare and it is possible that fights will erupt and damage to persons and property occur.   The following are typical of incidents occurring in the North Eastern Region of Newcastle upon Tyne, and possibly elsewhere in the UK, in which intoxication through sniffing has played a significant part.

   A number of youths had been glue sniffing since the end of
   school that afternoon.   They climbed onto the roof of a youth
   club and started pounding on the roof to attract the attention
   of those inside.   When the youth leader came out and asked them
   to stop one of the youths jumped down and punched him in the
   face causing a major incident in which the police had to be
   called.

   Two youths high on glue fumes were passing the premises of their
   secondary school.   They began to shout loud abuse at the school
   and memories of their teachers until one action led to another
   escalating to the point where they forced entry and started a
   fire which caused £35,000 worth of damage.

   A punk gang told of how they inhaled solvents to work up courage
   to commit burglaries.   Several of the group admitted attacking
   women and stealing their handbags whilst intoxicated.

   A 17 year old girl terrorised her mother and sister while
   intoxicated by glue fumes.   She would smash household items
   and furniture and threaten her relatives with knives and pokers
   to the point where they sometimes had to lock themselves in a
   room to avoid her until she had calmed down.   During these
   high states the girl would frequently beat her head against
   the wall shouting abuse and hatred towards her estranged
   father.   Sometimes the neighbours became so concerned that
   they telephoned for the police.

   A youth of 19 years, very much a loner, likes to steal cars
   and sniff from a glue bag while he is driving around.   On
   other occasions he drives his motor cycle, a 500 cc machine
   which is hardly roadworthy around the backstreets of his

home area terrifying all and sundry as he becomes steadily
more and more intoxicated from the glue fumes until
eventually he collapses unconscious.

Three boys and a girl were sniffing gas (butane lighter
refills) in a shed next to a cafe. Whilst they were all
high one of their number lit a cigarette just as another was
spraying gas from the aerosol can. The resulting explosion
cost £20,000 worth of damage and almost killed a mother and
young child who were on the other side of the cafe wall.
The sniffers were injured but survived.

A gang of skinheads tour the area looking for fire extinguishers
which they steal and use for sniffing purposes. They prefer
the small fire extinguishers from ambulances and omnibuses
which they take into tower flats to sniff. They jam open
lift doors and sniff around fires which they light in the
stairwells causing great fear to the inhabitants who are
mostly old age pensioners.

Older boys and girls who are truanting from comprehensive
schools lie in wait for younger children on their way home
from school and force them to sniff from glue bags.

As the above incidents reveal there are many aspects to the activities
of sniffers which spread alarm and anger through the local community.
In some cases the behaviour is so antisocial that the outcome is a
whole range of crimes which are linked with intoxication through glue
sniffing and the abuse of solvents. It is interesting in this respect
to examine the information in figure   which is a summary of the
court cases involving sniffing which were reported in certain listed
newspapers. Although the information presented is derived solely from
press cuttings which are prey to inaccuracies of many kinds it is
nevertheless an indication of the social problems especially delinquency
to which sniffing activities have been linked. In the absence of more
reliable and valid statistical surveys of the problem the information
given is worthy of attention for several reasons. For example, the
age ranges of the offenders for particular offences shows that sniffing
activities are indulged by young people beyond the middle teenage years
and this information further supports the idea that the attractions of
glue sniffing practices are beginning to involve progressively older
age groups. Another feature of this information worth noting is the
comparatively large number of thefts recorded. Many of these cases
involved actual thefts of solvents and volatiles for inhalation
purposes. Information culled from reports at the University
Counselling Clinic would confirm the trend in these statistics since
many sniffers maintain that they are able to steal products to sniff or
even items to sell in order to buy substances for sniffing purposes.

Further to the above it cannot be overstressed that sniffing can
cause serious damage to the young person's social development and
growth. Truancy rates in comprehensive schools in many parts of the
UK but especially the Northern Region appear to be at an all time high
judging from verbal reports by teachers although official figures are
hard to find. Such figures derive from a multitude of conditions
affecting pupils but among these sniffing abuses appear to be

35

NEWSPAPER REPORTS OF COURT CASES INVOLVING
VOLATILE SUBSTANCE ABUSE - 1980 to 1982

OFFENCE	NOs	AGE RANGE	MODE	SEX	VOLATILE SUBSTANCES INHALED
Theft	46	11 to 22	15	43M 3F	Petrol, Glue, Fire Extinguisher, Butane Gas
Breach of the Peace	28	14 to 20	17	26M 2F	Glue
Criminal Damage	14	14 to 20	16	13M 1F	Glue, Butane Gas
Burglary	13	14 to 22	16	13M	Glue, Butane Gas
Assault	13	15 to 22	15	13M	Glue
Arson	10	14 to 18	17	9M 1F	Glue, Nail Varnish
Rape	6	16 to 26	16	6M	Glue, Petrol
Receiving Stolen Goods	5	13 to 15	14	5M	Glue
Murder	4	15 to 18	15	4M	Glue
Threatening Behaviour	4	14 to 16	15	4M	Glue
Causing Actual Bodily Harm	3	17 to 18	17	3M	Glue
Wounding	3	16 to 18	17	3M	Glue
Possessing Explosives	3	15 to 16	16	3M	Glue
Driving under Influence of Solvents	2	24 to 30		2M	Glue
Driving under age	1	14		M	Glue
Joy riding	1	17		M	Glue
Section 5 Public Order Act	1	18		M	Glue
Contravening Army Act conduct prejudicial to Good order and Discipline	1	19		M	Glue
Carrying an Offensive Weapon	1	17		M	Glue

Figure 3.4

36

Causing Grievous Bodily Harm	1	15	M	Glue
Indecent Assault	1	16	M	Glue
Indecent Exposure	1	20	M	Glue
Culpable Homicide	1	16	M	Glue
Possessing Ammunition	1	17	M	Glue
Offence against Ecclesiastical Courts Jurisdiction Act 1860	1	18	M	Glue

TOTALS: 165 Offences - 158M 7F
          104 Court Cases

Approximately 90% of Volatile Substance inhaled were Glue Fumes.

Court Cases were heard in the following places:

  Belford, Rochdale, Hebburn, Gateshead, Hexham, Hartlepool, Peterlee,
  Wakefield, Bulford, Hexham, Newcastle upon Tyne, Berwick, Teesside,
  Hamilton, Glasgow, Blaydon-on-Tyne, South Shields, Derwentside,
  Shrewsbury, Wallsend, Calder, North Shields, Old Bailey, Blyth,
  Barnsley, Wigan, Cardiff, Kirkcaldy, Gosforth, Birmingham, Felling,
  Horsham, Consett.

Court Hearing involved Crown Court, Magistrates Courts and Juvenile
Panels.

The newspaper reports were published in the following:

  The Northumberland Gazette, Shields Gazette, Hexham Courant, The
  Newcastle Journal, The Daily Telegraph, Northern Echo, Daily Mirror,
  The Newcastle Evening Chronicle, The Berwick Advertiser, The
  Yorkshire Post, Shields Weekly News, The Sun, The Guardian, The
  Times, The Daily Express, The Daily Mail.

NB While every effort was made to check all the reported court cases
     involving volatile substance abuse the author recognises that there
     may be many reports which were not included in the above statistics
     which are merely to be taken as an indication of how sniffing
     activities may adversely affect Behaviour and cause problems within
     the community.

Figure 3.4

very important.   Reports from the sniffers themselves suggest that
there are many pupils who dodge going to school in order to join
sniffing parties or to sniff alone.   Individual cases at the
University Counselling Clinic indicate that not all pupils who truant
to sniff are poor school performers or even underachievers although the
majority appear to be.   It does seem to be the case that glue sniffing
is an attractive form of escape from the worries that many pupils have
about school as well as being a fashionable fad which is a challenge to
the authority of the school and society at large.   Unfortunately, the
situation is exacerbated in some schools where sniffers are suspended
when caught.   Two 15 year olds attending the University Counselling
Clinic told of a situation in which having been identified as habitual
sniffers by the school they were given their attendance mark when next
they went to school and then it was suggested to them that they should
leave.   The verbatim report mentioned a particular housemaster who was
obviously fed up with pupils disrupting his classes through glue sniffing
and had apparently said to these two hard cases:

> 'Well now you've got your mark you can both piss off and
> don't come near these buildings or the other kids again
> today'.

If this statement is true then it can only serve to reinforce the view
shared by many teachers and members of the general public alike that
schools are ill equipped generally to deal with teenage pupils who
develop emotional problems leading to behaviour disorders such as
volatile substance abuses.   McMaster (1982) has shown that traditional
attitudes to educational caring are becoming obsolete.   Glue sniffing
more than anything else has caused many teachers to look beyond the
academic rigidities of the traditional curriculum to find ways of
helping individual pupils to adjust to life's problems without the use
of intoxicants.

At home within the sniffer's family the problems raised are even more
serious.   At the University Counselling Clinic a mother talked of how
she lies awake until her 17 year old son returns home high on solvents.
She helps him to bed and then watches in case he vomits and chokes.
Once in the middle of a winter's night she searched the neighbourhood
for him and discovered that he'd collapsed unconscious in a garden
further down the street.   If she had not found him she believes he
might have died from the extremely cold temperatures that night.   Glue
sniffing is her nightmare because it threatens to take her son away for
ever.

In a similar way a father talked of how his beloved daughter had
changed out of all recognition since she had started inhaling glue
vapour.

> 'She used to be so loving and cheerful.   Happy and fresh.
> But now she looks scruffy and sick, she won't eat her food
> and she gives her mum and me a lot of cheek and backtalk which
> she never did before.   Just now she's suffering from a burn
> on her arm from when she reached into the fire because a voice
> in her head had told her to do it.   She's got her mum and me
> nearly nervous wrecks with worrying about her.'

Accounts such as the above are commonplace at the University Counselling Clinic where parents often come alone for advice about how to manage and help their youngsters who have become involved in glue sniffing. From such data as this it is possible to state quite emphatically that the inhalation of volatile substances not only disrupts normal patterns of social behaviour but it can impair and even arrest the individual's capacity to develop as a person. Because the overall effect of intoxication is to direct the attention of the individual inwards there is a consequent loss of contact with external reality. The sniffer begins to act in his problems through chemically induced phantasies so that he or she becomes unreachable even by formerly close relatives and friends. When an adolescent acts out his problems there is always a chance of interacting with him and establishing communication. But with chronic sniffers there is a withdrawal that often puts them beyond normal contact until they decide they want help.

It is interesting to reflect that when Glaser (1966) introduced a new clinical concept to the American Psychiatric Association which he labelled 'Inhalation Psychosis' he had in mind the manner in which the glue sniffer abuses his own person as a target for frustrations and agressions. By poisoning his system to the point where it ceases to remind him of the demands of a real world the sniffer is able to plunge into a crazy existence of his own making which his anaesthetised CNS is too weak to control and correct.

Consideration of the ill effects of sniffing on the social life of the individual presents a dismal picture of withdrawal into an isolated wasteland of mental aberration and curious phantasies which threaten to break the individual's tenuous hold on the realities of ordinary life. But for others in the community the activities of sniffers can become a menace which gives rise to fear and anger as the following anecdotes illustrate.

The headteacher of an urban infants school telephoned the author to ask for advice and help in relation to the problems which glue sniffers were causing at her school. She told of glue bags (plastic bags containing glue) which littered the playgrounds and which were being used by some of the infants in imitation of the glue sniffers they had seen in the streets adjoining the school. Matters had got worse recently when a six year old had been accosted on his way home from school by a group of glue sniffers. They had terrorised the youngster by spray painting his shoes and parts of his skin pink. The child had been so shocked that he suffered an asthma attack and had to receive hospital attention. Other children from the school had been similarly molested and some had been bullied into sniffing. Several children had become sick and vomitted as a consequence. In view of these happenings the head teacher and her staff had officially requested police protection for the children.

The other incident concerned old people living near a tower block of flats whose predicament highlights the vulnerability of the innocent whether child or adult to the whims of roving bands of intoxicated youths out for mischief and excitement.

Mrs. Williams is a widow of 69 years. She lives alone in an upstairs flat in a terrace that has seen better days. She is afraid to go to bed at night and sits in the lounge the whole night through with the lights on and a hammer by her side. Twice her front door was battered open. Once discarded glue bags were thrown up the stairs and set alight with newspapers. On another occasion two youths stinking of glue confronted her and demanded money. They also threatened to rape her and only left when her shouts and screams roused a neighbour, a 70 year old man who set his dog, a labrador, on the intruders. A police spokesman commenting on the incident remarked that it is difficult for the law to intervene because glue sniffing is not illegal and yet they are aware of how sniffers can intimidate the general public without actually committing an offence.

For a final indication of how far volatile substance abuse constitutes a sociable problem it is pertinent to refer to Joan, a 24 year old graduate trained social worker who works in an intermediate treatment unit. She gives an account of how in response to instructions she and a male colleague went out to look for glue sniffers to persuade them to come along to the unit and talk about their sniffing. They eventually tracked a group down to a hideaway under a road bridge spanning a busy dual carriageway. The sniffers had tied a rope to an overhead buttress and were taking turns to swing out over the roadway to the alarm of approaching traffic. As the social workers approached they were pelted with empty cans and other missiles until they were forced to retreat. As Joan said 'These kids didn't want to know, they were crazy, high on glue and risking their own lives as well as the lives of motorists and passengers using the roadway. We waited at a distance and eventually tracked some of them home but they flatly refused our help. What more can we do? Unless these kids commit a crime as the law stands at present we cannot intervene even to preserve health and protect lives.'

Such a dilemma of responsible professionals in child care is echoed in many similar accounts that have been told to the writer during lecturing visits to different parts of the UK where help is sought because of problems with sniffers in the area. The will to care for and help the young is abundantly present in both the general public and the caring services but the opportunity to care for sniffers is dependent upon their willingness to accept such care. The damaging effects of sniffing will persist unless society can find ways of acting more responsibly towards sniffers by conveying to them the potential consequences of their present behaviour and providing firm guidance which will help them to avoid or overcome these abuses. After all it is the natural disposition of most adults to cherish and nurture the young so that they may be protected by the wisdom of those with experience against threats to their survival from whatever source. It appears that sniffing practices can constitute such a threat.

PSYCHOLOGICAL DAMAGE

The effects of solvent abuse tend to be basically similar for all individuals involved in this abuse but a variation in the effects may occur according to the nature of such factors as age, personality, physique, the substance inhaled, the quantity inhaled and the length

of sniffing history.   A group of teenage girls describing their
experiences when 'on the glue' spoke of seeing 'little red and green
men darting about like fireflies'.   Some of them <u>heard</u> 'funny buzzing
and ringing sounds' and <u>saw</u> 'bright lights flaring'.   Others reported
feeling frightened and sick.   Some felt sexy feelings and wild abandon.
Feelings of aggression and wanting to smash things were frequently
experienced by the sniffers some of whom had also felt urges like
'wanting to walk out a window' and 'feel just like I could fly'.   Some
of the experiences reported by these young teenagers were extremely
nasty and included delirium tremens type experience ...

<u>Example</u>   'Everything went dark and there was this red light everywhere.
    Insects and horrible crawly things were all around and I could
    hear monsters moaning and coming nearer.   Something with a
    horrible face got hold of my neck and I was so scared I just
    screamed and screamed.   I got so frightened I wet myself'.

   One of the girls in care was discovered, whilst still suffering the
aftermath of a solvent sniffing episode, repeatedly crying out 'Get off
me', and she was whimpering and staring wild eyed at the floors and
walls of the room she was in and generally acting in a most terrified
manner.   This experience proved to be so frightening for her that even
a year afterwards she still spoke with fear about the experience.   It
seems that as the CNS becomes progressively intoxicated through the
inhalation of volatile hydrocarbons there begin to emerge distinct
psychological effects.   Ten years ago Wyse (1973) was able to describe
four identifiable stages of CNS depression each of which give rise to a
whole range of symptoms many of which figure largely in the sniffer's
psychological awareness.   These stages are summarised below.

   The first stage is called the excitatory stage which gives rise to
changes in mood towards feelings of euphoria, dizziness and excitement
and generally pleasant exhilaration.   It is at this stage that intense
visual and sometimes auditory hallucinations commonly occur.

   Psychological changes at the second stage result in confusion,
feelings of disorientation and loss of self control.   These feelings
are intensified at the third stage leaving the person in a dreamy
drowsy state which at the next stage, the fourth, gives way to loss of
normal awareness and the experience of vivid dreams.   The overall most
powerful psychological effect of sniffing is the induction of dream
states and hallucinations.   The composition of the sniffers'
hallucinations tend to vary with the person but all the sniffers
attending the University Counselling Clinic reported a variety of what
they referred to as ILLUSIONS.   For example: Lynn 15 years said
that when she was high on glue she often saw Dracula coming through
the wall to get her.

   'He was horrible, blood dripping from his mouth.   People were
    lying dead on the floor.   I went to see my brother and he was
    just a skeleton lying on the bed.   I ran in to see my sister
    and little sister who were just skeletons.   The house was all
    dark and black and there was just a little red light on in the
    ceiling and I could hardly see.   I was terrified'.

This example is a typical hallucinatory experience reported by sniffers. The pattern of hallucinations is fairly predictable among adolescent sniffers and seems to stem more from subjective factors than the pharmacological actions of the drug although there are some chemicals which can stimulate hallucinatory processes in the brain more than others. It is clear, however, that the majority of sniffers are attracted to these practices because of the hallucinations which are a rich source of enjoyment and excitement. It is important to recognise that the chemical fumes inhaled by sniffers are drugs in the sense of the definition by the World Health Organisation: 'A drug is a substance which when taken into the living organism may modify one or more of its functions'. The misuse of solvents is a form of drug taking as has been pointed out elsewhere (Tacade, 1983) and needs to be approached as such. As the case is with other drugs which alter conscious states of perception so the sniffer experiences mind altering experiences according to the relative influences of his background, personality and surroundings. In this respect it is interesting to find the hallucinations are less of an end in themselves than a means to an end. For the sniffer hallucinations serve a definite purpose. In some cases the purpose is to escape from unsatisfactory feelings such as the following case:

Richard, an 18 year old has been sniffing on and off for years. Unlike many other adolescent he is never any trouble when high and prefers to sniff alone. He presented at the University Counselling Clinic as a self referral case because his girl friend was beginning to complain about his glue sniffing. Richard said that he enjoyed sniffing because it helped him to forget his troubles and made him relax. At a later date he disclosed that during sniffing sessions he would often see his mother who had left home when he was 10 years old. He said that this hallucination gave him immense pleasure and he began to inhale glue fumes on a regular basis to see his mother again and to gain relief from the sense of loss that he still felt at times. A further remark by Richard at this stage revealed an interesting link between the hallucinations of his lost mother and the nature of his feelings about her. It emerged that his father had forbidden any mention of mother and had even removed photographs of her. When he was 17 years Richard had asked his father if he could have a photograph of his mother and he was refused. It is undoubtedly true that Richard indulged sniffing for many reasons but a significant reason appeared to be his wish to see his mother again.

As the above case of Richard shows the hallucinations experienced by sniffers can be sheer escapism and wish fulfilment. This understanding has important connections for treatment because of the clear insights offered into possible motivations and causes of sniffing.

With regard to those hallucinations which are frightening pictures such as monsters, ghouls and poisonous creepy crawlies it seems again that they partly answer a basic psychological need for emotional experience of the exciting kind. Many young people are morbidly curious about supernatural phenomena and the significance of death.

The increased psychological awareness of himself as a person is for the adolescent a spur to examine the world in relationship to his own feelings. The popular view of the happy truant is far from the truth in many cases and it is a matter of observation to find adolescents who should be in school, wandering the streets and shopping centres brooding on their feelings. A clue to the volatile nature of their feelings is indicated by the often present transistor radio or cassette recorder playing music which temporarily relieves and finds expression for acute stresses and strains. The glue bag, a rag saturated in solvents, or a spray can are devices which serve a similar purpose of emotional release, as illustrated by the following example from the Clinic.

Grace presented as an unhappy 17 year old. Bright intellectually she sees herself going either to College or University not because she wants to but because it is expected of her by the family. Since becoming involved with sniffing her performance in school subjects has deteriorated and she was under pressure to improve. During the interview she began to relax to the point where she felt able to remark: 'Everything in my home is so stale and tight. Nobody gets excited, nobody slams a door or swears or makes a noise or cries even, because my father will not allow it and my mother just goes along with him'.

What Grace was feeling was the normal healthy urge to express her emotions spontaneously without fear of condemnation from her parents. Denied this expression she resorted to inhaling butane gas from a lighter refill aerosol can.

As a result of CNS depression imagery appears to increase with the consequent personification of goodness and evil. Many sniffers report hearing voices in their heads which are often described as coming from God or the Devil. Pickens and Heston (1979) offer an interesting insight into hallucinations resulting from solvent misuse which they link with drug abuse generally.

In the light of their studies it follows that solvent abuse presents clinical symptoms of an acute hallucinatory nature featuring psychological effects such as clouding of consciousness, confusion and hallucinations of a threatening primitive kind. Further to this it is suggested that the chronic sniffer may suffer some rudimentary and temporary psychotic effects such as delusions and paranoia which emerge as strong feelings of jealousy, fearfulness and environmental threat. While it is carefully pointed out that the chronic abuse of solvents does not usually trigger prolonged states of psychosis there are potentially disturbing implications. It seems that unlike hallucinogenic drugs such as Cannabis and LSD, intoxication through volatile hydrocarbons does not usually stimulate self awareness of the drug induced state but prevents such awareness. Further it is observed that behaviour becomes progressively disinhibited with all the consequent dangers of this for the sniffer and those around him.

Reference to case studies at the University Counselling Clinic serves to confirm the above statements. Dorothy a young teenager in care at a community home with education on the premises (CHE) was admitted to the Royal Victoria Hospital Casualty Department in a highly intoxicated

43

state suffering from severe bruising and shock following a road accident in which a lorrydriver had almost killed himself trying to avoid her as she wandered aimlessly on a motor way overpass late one Sunday evening. Dorothy fearful of the response by staff at the CHE because her privileges might be withdrawn had panicked and given the writer's name to the Police when questioned since she had attended the Clinic for treatment on two occasions but never seriously. In hospital she had the following to say:

> 'The Police are lying, Mr. O'Connor. I was never near any motorway or any roadway. I was minding me own business just having a sniff and going about this field picking some lovely yellow and pink flowers and suddenly this bloody lorry was coming straight at me across the grass'.

There are many reasons important enough to Dorothy to tell lies to get herself out of a scrape but in these circumstances I was inclined to believe she was telling the truth. Partly because I knew her and she did not sound or look as if she was lying. Later as I was leaving the hospital one of the police officers told me that the lorry driver had mentioned in his statement that Dorothy:

> ' ... seemed out of this world. She was bending and picking things off the road and smiling all the time. She never even looked up when I blasted the horn'.

The Police had also retrieved a small plastic bag approximately one third full of glue near the spot where the accident had occurred. In another much publicised case involving George a sniffer who had several times turned up at the Clinic but refused treatment, savagely assaulted an old man walking his dog in the municipal park. George pleaded not guilty maintaining that he had been attacked whilst relaxing in the park by a space monster. Needless to say George was high at the time having consumed the vapour contents of a 500 ml. tin of glue which the Police recovered from the scene.

A final comment here is reserved for the authors of a paper entitled Plastic Cement, The Ten Cent Hallucinogen, who identified the potent effects of the fumes from plastic cements used by many children and adolescents in model making. The authors (Preble and Laury, 1967) point out that the deliberate inhalation of these vapours is an indication of psychological need to experience states of intoxication and seek refuge in a phantasy world. In a review of Solvent Abuse, Barnes, (1979), referred to findings that many more sniffers reported that they had been treated for psychological problems than non sniffers. Sniffers also appeared to have higher scores in tension discharge and anxiety inhibition tests than non sniffers. Masterton (1979) describes some sniffers as being psychologically determined to cope with under lying disorder and implies that solvents are to be viewed as a form of self medication to this end.

Ultimately consideration has to be given to how far the sniffer damages himself psychologically by behaving in ways likely to alienate him from the mainstream of the community in which he belongs. It is submitted, born out of the experience of caring for many sniffers, that the most serious psychological ill effect of volatile substance abuse

is the force of the habit itself. Once a person has discovered the
stress reducing effects of inhaling chemical fumes he is propelled by
the thrust of his own relief and pleasure to repeat such behaviour
again and again.   It may well be also, as some writers have implied,
notably D'Amanda et al (1977), that sniffers who develop dependency on
one drug may lose their discrimination against misusing other powerful
drugs.

The long term psychological effects of solvent abuse have been
analysed by a number of investigators notably Cohen (1977) who comments
that solvents may serve to introduce adolescents to a career of drug
dependence.   D'Amanda et al (1977), referred to above, found that
among Heroin addicts those who had a history of glue sniffing had on the
average abused more than twice as many substances as other addicts and
also that they were significantly more likely to have attempted
suicide possibly because they had developed less fear of dying when
compared to other heroin addicts.

Further to this there is evidence of physical dependence in certain
individuals who habitually sniff.   The chronic solvent abuser would
seem to develop tolerance which can be quite marked in individual cases
(Wyse, 1973) and exhibits withdrawal symptoms such as chills, delirium,
tremens, headaches, moderately severe abdominal pains and other
muscular cramps and hallucinations.   Substances in most common use
would seem to have the characteristic of increasing the level of
tolerance so that the abusers are obliged to increase the dosage in
order to achieve the same effects as previously, (UN Narcotics
Information, Mexico, 1977).   It has been suggested that habituation or
dependence appear to be related more to the degree of intoxication than
to the specific chemical inhaled, (Press and Done, 1967).   It follows
that although the solvents are not addictive the practice of solvent
inhalation is reinforcing and leads to habitual usage.   Research into
sleep patterns at Edinburgh, (Oswald, 1966), seems to be indicating
that there may well be physical withdrawal effects from what were
previously considered to be soft drugs, for example barbiturates and
amphetamines, (Watson, L.M. 1972)

Recent findings summarised by Dr. Heather Ashton (1983) on the nature
and extent of problems occuring through dependence on benzodiazephines
(tranquiliser) indicates that regular treatment (not abuse) for more
than a few weeks leads to both physical and psychological dependence in
some patients and that cessation of treatment can lead to a definite
drug withdrawal syndrome.   It may be that solvents and other volatile
substances could have similar effects which would explain the
appearance of the same type of withdrawal symptoms in some cases
attending the University Counselling Clinic.   Furthermore, it is
possible especially in the light of the above that in cases of volatile
substance inhalation there are physiological factors underlying the
psychological needs of habitual abusers.

Examination of the effects overall of volatile substance abuse leads
eventually to the question of 'who will willingly pay the bill for the
damage that is caused'.   Central government has traditionally
maintained a policy of non intervention.   The industries responsible
for producing volatile substances have tended to adopt sympathetic

attitudes to the problems of misuse but continued to manufacture and
retail these products unchanged and accrue the profits as a consequence
of their misuse. Many of the young sniffers who suffer some form of
disablement cost the authorities any sum from approximately £500 per
week to keep a child in residential care to £5,000 to give emergency
hospital treatment and aftercare to a sniffer admitted to casualty in a
coma or following an accident. In consideration of all the different
aspects of the effects of Volatile Substance Abuses mentioned above it
is clear that the organisation of effective caring responses to the
problem would, in the long term, have beneficial outcomes for the
economy as well as boosting the reputation of Government for
interventions carried out on humanitarian grounds.

4 CAUSES AND MOTIVATIONS

There are a multitude of possible causes and motives connected to
sniffing activities in every individual case.   The problem is
identifying the most significant agents which can be linked to the
specific behaviour in question without denying that there are others of
less importance.   Statistical surveys of population figures for
sniffing can provide a list in descending order of priority according to
the numbers involved.   The results of a small survey of this kind will
be mentioned later in this section and undoubtedly such research is
extremely useful in helping towards understanding the frequency and the
range of the factors involved.   But in determining the relative
influence of particular elements it is essential to consider the
subjective features entailed.   For it is at this level that the key
factors can be assessed with regard to finding an appropriate treatment
response.   It is the inner personal angle which is of vital substance
for the therapist.   In the light of what has been written above it is
interesting to consider the following.

The abuse, through deliberate inhalation, of glue and solvent vapours
by children and teenagers is remarkably similar to the adult usage of
alcohol and drugs when confronted with problems, frustration, anxiety
or crises.   With young people glue sniffing may take on the character
of a psychological crutch and become a coping mechanism which enables
the sniffer to avoid the harsh realities of day to day schooling and
living, (Kupperstein and Susman, 1968).   Writing about inhalant abuse
in an Indian Boarding School, Schottstaedt and Bjork (1977) commented
that for children denied the usual accoutrements of a home, toys,
personal possessions and reading materials, inhalation of solvents offered
solace, escape, entertainment, cameraderie, prestige and a degree of
personal gratification.   Peer groups pressure is a strong factor in
starting and maintaining the abuse, and in the majority of cases
sniffing is a group activity (Clements and Simpson, 1978).   Although
there are many cases of young people attending the University
Counselling Clinic who for various reasons choose to sniff alone.   Such
individuals are especially at risk and this element of danger may well
serve to partly motivate their isolated sniffing activities.

The question of why healthy young people indulge in mood changing and
mind warping practices such as glue sniffing and solvent inhalation is

not easy to resolve especially in view of comments such as the following from sniffers themselves:

'Because life is boring and frustrating'.
'It's exciting because it's dangerous'.
'It's something that parents and teachers don't like'.
'Because it makes you forget'.
'It makes me feel good'.
'You can get away from all your troubles'.
'Because my friends do it'.
'No reason, it was just something to do'.

These are some of the typical answers given by young teenagers. It may be that these answers are the really meaningful ones and that it is unnecessary to probe further, or it may be the trully valid reasons are not available to articulation and are submerged in the individual's mind. Whatever the explanation may be the fact remains that there is a problem presenting in our homes and our schools, (Watson, L.M., 1972).

It seems that any product containing solvents will be abused for 'kicks' irrespective of objectionable odours or the degradation of having to steal the substance, (Cohen, 1977). Most of the products misused are easily available and are packaged in a convenient container suitable to fit into a coat pocket or handbag ready for instant use. Due consideration needs to be given to the view that both the insecure pupil who under-achieves and the materially better off social occasion abuser represent a significant element of passive protest which may stem from the inability to communicate with adult authority figures, (Kupperstein & Susman, 1968). Among the multitude of motivations influencing the glue sniffer is the sense of challenge and abandon. Even although the deliberate abuse of solvents is not illegal there is still such a strong feeling of self-indulgence about it that implies that, inevitably, public opinion will tend to be outraged. It may be significant with regard to motivation to observe that most studies have found that boys far outnumber the girls in this malpractice, Glaser and Massengale,(1962; Brozovsky and Winkler (1965); Watson, (1982).

Various reasons are advanced for this discrepancy but it would be misleading to simply conclude that boys are more attracted to sniffing volatile fumes than girls, for example Watson reports a projection of 4.8 : 1. It is worth considering that there may be other factors at work. First of all it must be pointed out that where glue sniffing and solvent abuses have started in all girl populations, such as those found in residential care establishments like community home schools with education on the premises, the figures for involvement have been as high as 75% (O'Connor, 1983). Also girls tend to be more skilled than boys at concealing the practice. For example, girls at the University Counselling Clinic said that they often used paper tubes or toilet roll holders to sniff through so that there would be less chance of getting sores and burns on their mouths and faces. Some girls said that they preferred to sniff gas (butane) because it did not have the disadvantages of glues which leave a smell on the breath and stain the clothing. Perhaps the most cogent reason of all is that girls are more vulnerable to abuse and attack when intoxicated than boys. It must also be recognised that, questions of sexual equality apart, for

the male it is often classed as a mark of esteem to have been highly
inebriated. It is a macho image. Whereas for girls it is usually
considered to be unfeminine to appear highly intoxicated. Perhaps
this would explain why there are more boys identified as sniffers in
mixed population figures but large percentages of girls found sniffing
in all girl samples as in residential care. Where the self image is
poor as often is the case with many young people in care there would
appear to be a greater likelihood that given the chance sniffing will
take place. It seems that on close scrutiny especially of adolescent
populations in care, girls are every bit as likely to sniff as boys but
usually tend to be less obvious about it.

A further influencing factor is the age of those involved. The
evidence seems to indicate an average age of 14 to 15 years for glue
sniffers, (Wyse, 1973), although children as young as six years have
been referred for medical attention in Glasgow (Watson, 1977). It
seems that the usual age range is from 8 to 17 years of age which
identifies solvent abuse as a problem of early and late adolescence even
although some adults, notably those serving prison sentences, also
indulge. Unlike many adolescent fads solvent abuse might serve as an
introduction to a career of drug dependence, (Cohen, 1977; D'Amanda et
al, 1977). If glue sniffing behaviours are analysed at the superficial
level then it becomes clear that all teenagers not just the
psychiatrically lame are potentially threatened by such simple
motivating forces as 'curiosity' and 'mimicking behaviour' which may
serve to explain why the practice tends to spread so fast.

Significant indications regarding the motives underlying solvent abuse
may emerge from a scrutiny of the personality characteristics of
habitual abusers. Although the consensus of opinion is that it is not
possible to describe a personality type which is typical of the solvent
abuser nonetheless attention may usefully be directed towards those
psychological characteristics which identify pupils at risk. In this
respect reference is being made to the chronic abuser, the habitual
sniffer who presents as an atypical child. Nearly all chronic abusers
of solvents seem to have difficulty in expressing basic emotions
associated with aggressive and/or sexual feelings, (Lewis and Patterson,
1974). The personality patterns of chronic users was found to be
similar to those of adult alcoholic patients (Massengale et al, 1963),
while Brozovsky and Winkler, (1965), in a study of hospitalised
adolescent glue sniffers, found that over half of the children were
suffering from psychotic conditions. Sokol (1965) in his study of
young sniffers described the typical glue sniffer as a boy of small
physical stature suffering from inferiority feelings and lack of self
esteem and it was suggested that the euphoria produced during solvent
inhalation temporarily alleviated these feelings and would therefore
tend to be reinforced.

A number of studies have linked glue sniffing with young people from
sub standard environments and the all too familiar index of emotional
and material deprivation. Barker and Adams (1963) found that most
glue sniffing boys came from a one parent family, in most cases the
mother. In a similar vein Massengale et al (1963) found a direct
relationship between glue sniffing and delinquency, a finding which
others support notably Watson (1977) who described solvent sniffing as

a group activity closely associated with high rates of truancy and poor scholastic performance. It seems that there tends to be a clustering of sniffers caused by peer group pressure within certain schools and in relation to specific geographical areas. Although as Cohen (1977) points out not all inhalant abusers are from low income families. Recent case study analyses in one London Borough indicate that in almost every case of persistent sniffing there had been marital problems between the parents and/or long standing difficulties in family relationships (Merrill, 1978).

Many of the recorded cases of solvent abuse which come to the attention of the authorities such as health, social services, education and the police, appear to be children and young persons who are already in the care of the local authority which indicates that certain levels of emotional and social deprivation may be determining factors. From what the young glue sniffers themselves say it would seem that the practice affords a form of social activity which caters for the needs for acceptance, status and regard for those children and teenagers who feel lonely, rejected or friendless. It seems that sniffing is mainly a group activity which is undoubtedly governed by peer group pressures and there may at times be an element of subversion in the activities due to leadership hierarchies and bullying. The available case work research indicates that some individuals are sufficiently motivated to inhale glue despite the risks involved.

A significant fact to emerge overall from a review of the literature on solvent abuse by the young is the implication for child care that the sniffers and the inhalers are reacting to the absence of a much needed degree of mother and father loving care and attention, (see review by Press and Done, 1967). Where a child or teenager feels this deprivation he or she is impelled to explore substitutes and may become 'hooked' on inhaling solvents. The prognosis then is a familiar one of increasing social isolation and withdrawal characterised by truancy and poor educational performance (Watson, 1977), self destructive behaviour (Schottstaedt and Bjork, 1977), behaviour disorders and social maladjustment (Clements and Simpson, 1978), and delinquency (Lewis and Patterson, 1974; Watson, 1979). It is suggested with some authority (Silberberg and Silberberg, 1974) that solvent abuse by children can precipitate a 'drug somino effect' which has been indicated by many cases at the University Counselling Clinic who report using tablets and pills of various kinds, as well as grass (cannabis), to provide variety to and often to heighten the effects of sniffing.

Further to the above an explanation of sniffing behaviour which failed to examine the physiological mechanisms involved would be in danger of missing the possible links with psychological factors operating on the sniffers awareness. In this way crucial elements of motivation and causation could be ignored or underestimated and therefore certain approaches to treatment might not be attempted. In view of this the following information and analysis is presented as relevant to the better understanding of sniffing behaviour.

BREATHING FOR LIFE

In ordinary circumstances a person will eat at least three times a day
but will breathe approximately 15 to 20 times per minute and at the end
of each day each individual will have inhaled approximately 23,000 pints
of air.*   The relative importance of the act of breathing in connection
with survival is clearly established by the truth of the statement : we
breathe to live and we depend on breathing to go on living.   Considered
at a fundamental level breathing is the first behaviour of the individual
which is associated with living independently of mother in the real
world.   It is significant here to note that the emotions appear to be
closely linked with respiratory activities as shown by the variations in
breathing rates which accompany strong feelings ranging from the extremes
of fear and anger to feelings of calm and relaxation.   It seems that
the individual's awareness of breathing is vitally related to how he
feels about life.   At an early age some children develop a
physiologically close association between breathing rate and the onset
of anxiety which is demonstrated by breath holding spells sometimes up
to the point of unconsciousness.   The precipitating factors in such
cases would appear to be mild injuries, frustration or fright and the
factor of surprise seemed to be important (Lombrose and Lermon, 1967).
Such breathholding attacks it was noted tended to cease spontaneously
at or before school age although fainting attacks in adulthood were a
frequent sequel of breathholding attacks in infancy.

From the point of view of volitional behaviour it is often observed by
schoolteachers that children play games of 'breathholding' sometimes to
the extreme of losing consciousness for a few seconds.   It is
interesting also in this context to refer to cases of asthma which often
develop during childhood through an involuntary link between emotional
states and breathing difficulties triggered by stress inducing
situations.

Whatever the physiological and psychological mechanisms may be which
are involved in the behaviours described above it seems certain that
there is a strong link between breathing and feeling tone for the
individual.   When the element of narcosis is introduced through
breathing intoxicants it could be that the physiological mechanisms
referred to above become part of the complexity of causes which
determine the continuance of sniffing activities.   The similarity
between the outcomes of breathholding and sniffing intoxicants such as
loss of consciousness and the link between feelings and the behaviour is
clearly evidenced.   This relationship merits further investigation if
only for the possibilities of finding other aids to therapy.   Here it
is sufficient to comment that the common denominator which
characterises many of the different inhalation abuses is the activity
of respiration.   It is necessary therefore to examine carefully what
appears to be happening in relation to the activities of breathing when
sniffing practices are indulged.

* Amcor's 'Modulon Air Ioniser' 1981, Roncastle London Ltd.

STAGES TOWARDS INTOXICATION THROUGH INHALING

The respiratory system is especially vulnerable to the introduction of toxicants from the external environment as already mentioned. As a method of achieving intoxication, inhalating through the mouth is the quickest natural means by which chemicals can be introduced into the bloodstream. The immediate effects achieved by inhaling toxic substances is a distinctive feature of the method. It brings instant relief from stress and pleasure. There is an awareness of an effect having taken place and a deceptive feeling of being in control together with a misleading impression that it is possible to stop that effect which is a result of impaired judgment due to intoxication. For the person it seems that at least a part of the activity of inhaling is under conscious control although this is illusionary. Allied to this feeling is the knowledge that breathing is essential to survival. Therefore to intervene in the breathing act is to interfere with the life force itself and perhaps to obliterate it. There is an excitement to be gained through tampering with the very basis of man's existence possibly to achieve greater control and also to change life for the better. Dependency becomes inevitable because of the euphoria achieved through intoxication. Frequently it is reported by young people at the University Counselling Clinic that they feel they can control the dependency on inhalants to the point where they strike a balance: this far and no further. 'I can give up whenever I like', they say. Unfortunately the illusionary nature of these sentiments becomes painfully apparent when treatment commences.

Stated in the simplest terms sniffing behaviour begins with an individual who wants to inhale for whatever reason. Having started sniffing he experiences a range of feelings which tend to reinforce the practice such as the euphoric effects, the security of being part of a group of sniffers with the attendant sense of belonging, and the status of being someone special, that is a Glue Sniffer. Further to this is the feeling of being identified with what is considered to be fashionable and yet risqué.

CASE STUDIES

A major difficulty in responding initially to cases of solvent abuse is that many professionals become unduly concerned with the symptoms which are presented. Another approach is favoured in which emphasis is concentrated upon the feelings and attitudes of the person who is indulging solvent intoxication activities for a multitude of reasons which cannot be simply explained away by reference to symptoms. The following case studies are intended to illustrate the extent to which underlying conditions are linked to inhalation abuses beyond the mere details of the presenting problems although the reader is left to draw conclusions regarding the degree to which such abuses can be attributed to anyone of the many facets presented.

Lynn is 15 years old. The first occasion on which she recalls sniffing occurred one night in October when she was at home. Lynn was sitting in the kitchen in her night attire prior to going to bed when her mother's male friend who was living with them at the time made a critical comment about Lynn's appearance. An argument developed during

the course of which Lynn's mother supported her boy friend's criticism
against Lynn. The outcome was that Lynn was forcibly evicted from the
house and left in the backyard clothed only in her nightdress and
slippers to contemplate her predicament. She said that she did not
feel unduly perturbed because she wore a secret key to the rear door
around her neck for just such emergencies, (a comment which indicated
that this was not the first time that this had happened). She waited
shivering in the shelter of an outhouse until all lights in the house
went out and then letting herself in she quickly dressed and left.
During the days that followed until she was eventually arrested and
returned home, Lynn begged a bed wherever she could and 'sniffed' glue
every day. A friend had introduced her to the practice and she has
used it ever since, whenever her feelings threatened to overwhelm her.

. . .

Joyce has never felt that anyone loved her. She is extremely
demanding and critical of others. When she left school she felt a
failure and blamed the teachers and her parents for everything. For
the last two years she has regularly sniffed a variety of substances
including the fumes from glue, nail varnish remover, typing eraser
fluid, paint thinner, butane gas lighter aerosol and felt tip marker
pen fluid. Lately she has been attending a College of Further
Education and has found her sniffing activities have been the cause of
trouble at the college. She did not respond easily to treatment
because it seemed she really did not want to contemplate a life in
which she could not 'get high to feel normal', she said.

Eventually her mother was persuaded to attend the Clinic (Joyce's
father is dead having died when she was 8 years old). In this case
what the mother had to say was most revealing and helped a lot in the
treatment we were able to design for her. It seems that when Joyce's
mother was pregnant her own mother frightened her with some exaggerated
tales of suffering during childbirth to such an extent that she refused
to go into hospital to have Joyce. As events transpired she ended up
one night having her baby in a cramped bedroom on a large double bed
covered by a soft mattress and with two amateur midwives in attendance.
The birth did not go well and as the mother's worst fears materialised
she became more rigid and her muscles locked the baby in. In due
course a General Practitioner was sent for who succeeded in delivering
the baby unharmed but the mother was left hurt and shocked so much that
she could not bear to hold her child. For a month it seemed, by her
account, the baby cried incessantly in spite of the ministrations of the
father and summary lady relatives. In desperation a doctor was called
and the baby was given sedation (Joyce's mother said phenobarbitone) to
relieve her crying and to ease the mother's nerves who had still not
mothered her baby.

Joyce is remembered as a difficult child given to temper tantrums in
which she appeared to stop breathing and lose consciousness. At the
age of 11 years she was discovered drunk from a bottle of sherry wine
she had half consumed. Since then there has been a succession of
drunkeness on alcohol and intoxication through solvents. Significantly
when asked if her mother loved her Joyce replied, 'I don't know. I'm
not sure, I think that she does not love me'. Her mother on the other
hand protests that Joyce, her only child, is adored.

. . .

Bob has been in and out of care since he was 4 years old.   Lately he
has been staying with his mother and stepfather and attending the local
comprehensive school.   His behaviour is violent.   At home he has a fit
of rage every time his stepfather reprimands him.   He has broken
mirrors and windows, once he set fire to the curtains in his bedroom and
had to be dragged from the smoke filled room.   Sometimes he stays with
his real father who has also remarried and there his behaviour is much
the same.   Recently he attacked his stepmother and assaulted the new
edition to his father's family, a three month old boy child.   Bob seems
to be torn apart by feelings for his divorced parents and his rage
erupts to dangerous outbursts of temper in which he threatens to kill.
His long term sniffing activities were brought to light when he was
admitted to hospital in a semi conscious state suffering from what his
mother thought was a 'nervous fit' but it was later established he'd
been inhaling hair spray directly from an aerosol.   He confessed to
having sniffed various volatile substances for some years, as far as he
could recall he first started shortly after his parents separated and he
was sent to stay with his grandmother.   Commenting on that time he
remarked that he felt lonely and abandoned.

                                  . . .

    Barbara says that she first started sniffing when she was 14 years of
age.   It was at the time she was courting an older boy and they used to
sniff together.   At sixteen Barbara gave birth to a son but was judged
to be unfit to mother him and he was taken into care although she
refused to sign adoption papers.   Whilst staying at a hostel for
unmarried mothers Barbara started sniffing again to forget 'John, her
baby'.   She had stopped sniffing during the pregnancy on medical
advice so as not to harm the baby.   At 17 years of age she was admitted
to hospital in a coma having been found under a stairwell in a shopping
centre by guard dogs.   She had apparently consumed vast amounts of glue
vapour.   It was later estimated the contents of four 250 ml tins.   At
the third attempt to insert a tube into her respiratory tract to enable
her to breathe she recovered consciousness.   For days afterwards she
complained bitterly and said that the doctors ought not to have saved
her life.   Barbara says that life without John is just not worth
living.

                                  . . .

    A social worker asked the author to accompany him on a visit to a
family who complained about the glue sniffing activities of their son,
Michael.   The house where they lived is a pleasant semi-detached
residence in one of the better parts of town.   There were two cars in
the driveway which adjoined a pleasant well kept garden.   The father
showed us into the hall heavy with the smell of glue.   In the lounge
Michael, a gloomy looking 15 year old sat slumped on the settee, head
buried in his hands, long black hair hanging down.   His father, a
professional man, stood over him like an avenging angel, gesturing
assertively as he held out Michael's glue bag for us to see and accused
his son of umpteen misdemeanours including truancy, laziness,
disobedience, dirty habits and, most serious of all, glue sniffing.
As we listened to him it was enlightening simply to tune in to the non
verbal communication between the different family members.

Mother, a stout forty, perched on the edge of the settee like a brown partridge in tweeds, staring sadly all the while at the dejected figure of her son and dabbing her eyes with a white lace handkerchief to relieve her stress. Occasionally she interjected quietly almost to herself 'We've done everything for him. But he lets everybody down. Why, oh why?', and the muted weeping began again. Father looked disapprovingly at the scene, tall and thin, immaculately dressed in a white shirt with a sensible tie, light trousers sharply creased and tan shoes polished to a hard shine. He was a picture of middle class elegance. He stood in the middle of the room dominating all around him now and then as if to punctuate his words his right forefinger would stab the air in the direction of his son. Michael seemed frozen as if he hardly dared to move in case he would upset somebody. He just sat there, a long thin gangly adolescent boy, ungainly and awkward looking. Dressed entirely in black he gazed fixedly at the floor with dark brooding eyes. 'Nobody loves me', his whole body posture said resignedly. Suddenly the door to the lounge swung open and in walked Michael's sister, a 10 year old vision of blonde blue eyed loveliness in a light dress clutching a poodle puppy. Father's countenance immediately softened and mother, startled, exclaimed, 'Samantha darling don't come in here you'll only get upset'.

The dynamics were all too clear to both of us. We now needed to articulate them sufficiently for this family to help them to ease the wretchedness of their son's predicament. It took a long time to change some of the ways in which this family behaved. Michael's glue sniffing seemed only incidental to these changes.

. . .

One Saturday morning in summertime the author went into the Clinic earlier than usual. There huddled on the steps was a blonde teenager in a thin dress and skimpy cardigan, fast asleep. Later when she had warmed herself at the gas fire and had consumed two cups of coffee heavily sweetened with sugar she told of how the Samaritans had talked her through the night when she had threatened to kill herself. It was they who had directed her to the Clinic after she had runaway from home. Her story touches upon a form of abuse and assault against children and teenagers which is reported, all too often, but which is frequently concealed and 'kept within the family'.

Anne, as she was called, sniffed glue fumes regularly but especially at weekends when she aimed to achieve oblivion through intoxication. Her mother, a divorcee, was living with a man who had a son in his early twenties who usually stayed with them at weekends. It was often the case on Fridays and Saturdays that all the adults got drunk and it had become common practice for the two men to visit Anne's bedroom and use her as a sexual plaything. Anaesthesia through solvent vapour intoxication was the only way she knew of making the outrages she suffered bearable. 'Screaming only made them do worse things', she said, 'so glue was my only friend'. Anne was just 14 years old at the time. Mercifully she was rapidly released into local authority care as soon as the professional caring services could be formally mobilised. In the interim period, the reader might care to know, a bed was found for her in a place of safety. Subsequently there were no reports of her sniffing but she continued to attend the Clinic for counselling for some time afterwards.

. . .

A recurring theme in all the case profiles listed here is the force of
the individual's feelings in providing the motive power for sniffing
intoxicants.   Another notable feature of many cases not just those
described above is that the emotional power which stimulates and
sustains sniffing activities seems chiefly to be feelings of the
negative kind.   Such feelings are frequently the outcome of conditions
like the following:

> hurts through rejection by parents and relatives; constant
> criticism from teachers; inability to perform according to
> expectations in school; failure in personal relationships;
> boredom and frustration in the absence of established work,
> recreation, and leisure routines; self consciousness and
> worries about personal popularity and being attractive to
> the opposite sex.

Although imitation of peers, curiosity and the enduring pursuit of
pleasure also figure largely in sniffing practices especially when they
are just beginning it does appear that from the individual cases
reviewed at the Clinic it is chiefly anxiety provoking feelings, as for
example the negative feelings listed above, which seem to fuel sniffing
abuses to levels beyond the superficial and experimental.

Comments from young people involved in Volatile Substance Abuse

To research the facts about glue sniffing it is necessary to consult the
practitioners themselves.   Most of those involved in sniffing abuses to
a chronic level are guarded about their activities until such time as
they feel they need help when the tendency is to talk openly about why
they do it irrespective of the ill effects experienced.   What follows
is taken from actual verbatim reports of sniffers attending the Clinic.
They are given without comment since they have a clear message of their
own and relate closely to what has already been written.

The story of a Glue Sniffer by Barry
(14 year old pupil at a comprehensive school)

I first sniffed glue one morning at about 7.30 a.m.   It was in my
father's shed where he had a jar of it.   So I took a plastic bag and
put some glue in it.   At first I hesitated and smelt it once or twice
then remembering how other people had told me how to do it I inhaled
some glue.   At first I thought nothing was happening then the sounds
of everything seemed to get closer and faster and I remember sitting and
listening to them.   Then there was this buzzing in my ears like
helicopters coming and lights started flashing in front of my eyes and
I got sick and vomitted.

Then I placed more glue in the bag and inhaled it even faster but this
time I got a tingling all over and I must have passed out because I
remember nothing about that time.

Then after a few days school became boring and I started to think
about what I had done.   I knew another sniffer in our school so I told
him I had tried it and I knew where I could get some glue.   So we both
sneaked out of school and headed for the glue in my father's shed.   And
we took it and it was great.

56

A few days later he said why don't we try some evostick out of the
proper tubes.   So we chipped in for it and took it.   It was even
better than the other stuff, maybe it was stronger but there was more
colours and more better feelings, and no ill effects.   After that we
kept taking it and I took it by myself.   I bought more glue and it
progressed from there.   It was lovely when I sniffed because I could
forget everything.

Now I feel I need it, but I don't want to.   I keep smelling it;
getting dreams about it and sort of crave for it.   But now, since I've
set my mind on stopping, these things have got worse.

. . .

Yvonne (13 year old pupil in city school)

Author: 'Tell me Yvonne, in your own words, why you started to sniff
          glue fumes, how did that come about?'

Yvonne: I was sick of my life because my mam and dad were always
          arguing and fighting.   Then they were splitting up and my
          mam left home.   My dad went away and there was nobody to
          look after us except my big brother.   I did not really get
          on with my big brother, he was always hitting my big sister
          and me - so I just started to sniff.   The glue made me feel
          a lot better.

Author: Did you sniff with anyone else?

Yvonne: Sometimes this boy from down our street would come up to me
          and ask for some glue.   I could tell he wanted it badly
          because if I would not give him some he would sit down and
          cry.   When I gave him some it was like he was dying to get
          at it.

. . .

Poem by Corinne (15 year old pupil at a comprehensive school)

I'm a deprived kid,
And no one loves me,
So I turn to my glue bag,
To make me happy

It is the one thing,
I look forward to, '
To escape from reality,
and it's easy to do

I sniff it by night time,
I sniff it by day,
and then all my problems,
slip right away

But then my poor glue bag,
It splits at the seams,
And I'm left with reality,
and all it's bad dreams

To solve all these problems,
I buy some more,
And kick reality,
Out the back door

Some say I'm crazy,
Some say I'm mad,
But to hide from reality,
Ain't all that bad

All the good times have gone,
And I'm left as one,
So I have no reason,
To go on

Comments by this girl written as doodles on a piece of paper while being counselled.

Dad, hated for life for being a home breaker.
Death to dad.
Death to the leper (her father).

. . .

Finally an extract from a letter to a woman counsellor at the Clinic from Kathleen an 18 year old jobless teenager.

'I won't be coming into the clinic no more because there is no point because I've decided that I'm better on the glue than off. I went on the glue on Wednesday and I felt much better. I was off the glue for five weeks but things were getting worse instead of better. My mam thinks just because I don't tell her things no more that I'm alright. Well she's very wrong.

By the way I went up my dad's about 3 weeks ago to make friends but it didn't work out. He really couldn't care less. I wish I never went now. I really hate him. He's a bastard. Me and my mam even don't get on. I'm not bothered really.

On Monday it was a bad day, in fact it was a bloody terrible day. I woke up in a bad mood and I got bored then I had my cravings for the glue so I went on it in the afternoon (I put it off for a couple of hours though which is a miracle). If I didn't sniff I would kill myself so I might as well sniff. I'll probably end up walking the streets soon because this place is driving me mad. I've had about enough of this place. I say thanks a lot for the help you and Denis gave me. I always learn the hard way anyway. Tell Denis thanks a lot for wasting his time on me.'

. . .

The Parents View

For many parents there is an experience of shock at finding out about a daughter or son's involvement in sniffing abuses. Adults generally it seems from parents reactions at the Clinic find it difficult to understand why young people should want to inhale evil smelling substances at all.   As one parent commented:

> 'I had no idea that she was sniffing until I found all these
> empty gas lighter refills under her bed.   It hurt me to think
> that my daughter could do such a thing to herself.   I wanted
> to hurt her for being so stupid and in fact I did punish her
> but it had no effect.   She says it's her life and she'll do
> as she pleases.   I feel helpless about it.   I don't know
> where to turn'.

The feelings expressed by this mother are by no means exceptional and
deserve our sympathy and help yet they illustrate a curious kind of
ambivalence.   For example, many parents of children and teenagers who
inhale intoxicants are themselves dependent on chemicals for relief from
anxiety and stress.   Some of the fathers and mothers who are so
critical at the Clinic of their youngsters sniffing activities,
regularly consume alcohol for pleasure until they becom inebriated.
Each year there are millions of pounds worth of tranquilisers and
sleeping tablets used by a general public who seem strangely horrified
when teenagers are seen to intoxicate themselves in a similar fashion.
In everyday life there is a mute acceptance of the drug seller's
message whether it is advertising alcoholic beverages or headache
relieving pills.   All about us the media carries a message promising
relief and happiness through the use of chemicals.   Is it really any
wonder that young people feel like sampling some of this pleasure for
themselves?   Is it not surprising, that adult advice which says 'do as
I tell you not as I do' is ignored?   A teenager attending the Clinic
put it succinctly when he said:

> 'Look here my mother takes pills for everything: her nerves, to
> get to sleep, to cheer her up and she even took some pills before
> she sat her driving test and yet more pills when she failed.   My
> father boozes at the pub every night.   Why shouldn't I have
> something?'

Further to the above sentiment a point often made about alcohol abuse
which is even more applicable to solvent abuses by adolescents is the
feeling that unless they take something to intoxicate themselves their
lives will be unbearably dull.   For lots of teenagers therefore the
normal practice when party going or having a night out is to inhale and/
or drink intoxicants.   The principle implied by this behaviour is that
without the euphoria of inebriation there can be no enjoyment.

Commenting on adolescent disturbances as a reflection of family
relationships Shorter, (1975), suggests that life within the presentday
family seems to be evolving in directions which have no historical
precedent, the result of which is a severing of the lines of communication between the younger and older generations.   The implications made
here is that there are a number of factors which appear to adversely
affect adolescent behaviour and it is relevant here to refer to these as
possible causes of sniffing problems.   Stated briefly they are:

Instability in the life of the married couple.   The high rate of
divorce has led to upsetting situations for many adolescents which is all
the more confusing since as the statistics reveal, divorce seems to be a
way of changing partners with remarriage in mind which does not

necessarily indicate an anti marriage stance.   But the emotional lives
of the offspring can be so disrupted as to precipitate crises which may
damage the individual's capacity for making close relationships.

Cutting the links between the younger and the older generations
already referred to in which the adolescent can be left feeling very
much alone without clear cut standards of behaviour which he can
selectively both challenge and adapt within his own life style.   A
result of this has been a noticeable reduction of parental influence in
favour of the peer group.

The destruction of the warm cosy family nest notion which has arisen
because women in this age of equal rights are not so prepared to devote
their services in the traditionally selfless way.   Economic factors may
also contribute to the need for both parents to work with the result
that there is less time and energy for special family needs.   Among
these latter and considered to be essential for the maintenance of
stability, harmony and happiness within the family scene is the element
of loving care and attention.   Young people at whatever stage of their
development need to be cherished and prized for themselves alone.   They
thrive on unconditional love and attention.   Without it the deprivation
syndrome so familiar to professionals in child and adolescent care
begins to develop with the inevitable consequence that young people
begin searching for a means of escape from discomforting feelings of
neglect and rejection.

For the adolescent the impairment of relationships within the family
due to rapid social changes referred to above in terms of Shorters'
study can lead to the development of what has been defined by writers
from Durkheim onwards as a state of anomie in which the individual,
according to Plant (1975), experiences a state of spiritual sterility
and becomes responsive only to himself or herself and is responsible to
no one, 'He lives on a thin line of sensation between no future and no
past'.   Carried to extremes it is possible to share with Robins and
Cohen (1978) their concern over the significance of the Stretford End
Chant 'We hate humans', as one of the most poignant indications of the
deranged moods suffered by sections of the youthful population.   A line
from the song made popular by the Pink Floyd group 'Hey teachers, leave
us kids alone', (1980) is perhaps a firm indication from pupils, who are
after all the consumers, that our schools are not the sheltered and
caring places they are put out to be.   Without the security and support
which is ordinarily provided within family, school and community the
young person becomes increasingly isolated from developing a realistic
life style and may therefore feel tempted to escape to the relative
fulfilment of a chemically induced phantasy world.

A THEORY OF VOLATILE SUBSTANCE ABUSE

The available literature within the social sciences is noticeably
deficient in a theoretical structure to explain the deliberate
inhalation of volatiles to achieve intoxication by children and
adolescents.   A synthesis of all the identifiable features affecting
causation and motivation would provide the basis for a theory of
attribution to clarify the dynamics involved.   Krasowski, (1979)
has already attempted to formulate such a theory in which he refers

60

chiefly to the negative influences operating in some families which deny
the sniffer the security and freedom in which to grow as a person. The
result is an individual with a poor self concept who becomes
increasingly burdened with inferiority feelings particularly as
authority figures from the home, the school, the law and the community
react adversely to his sniffing. For the sniffer it is rewarding to
receive so much substitute attention from his activities which
temporarily relieves the anxieties associated with the home environment
and social interactions. Further, intoxicating effects of sniffing
volatiles is disinhibiting which tends to alleviate feelings of
inadequacy but can develop a dependency on the intoxicating syndrome.
Additionally there is reference to evidence implying that today's
sniffers are tomorrow's addicts whether it is addiction to alcohol or
drugs.

   Central to this theory is the notion that there is a distinct pattern
of behaviour which characterises the habitual sniffer to the extent
that it becomes an habitual observance or even a career. The behaviour
profile which emerges is essentially that of a young person who spends a
lot of time each day carrying out a series of rituals connected with
sniffing. For the chronic sniffer who may expect to lose consciousness
for a while or at least be rendered inoperative there is the problem of
finding a safe place to indulge the activities of inhaling without fear
of interruption. Since sniffers hideouts are frequently uncovered by
police patrols acting on complaints from the general public, there is
the excitement for the individual, either acting alone or within a
small group, of searching out a sniffing den. Popular places which
vary according to the weather conditions tend to be out of the way areas
like municipal parks, cemeteries, common wasteland, tips and dumps of
abandoned cars, unused railway lines and sidings, derelict buildings and
boarded up public conveniences although new building sites and the
emergency staircases of tower blocks with lifts have also been used.

   In addition there is the problem of finding a supply of volatile
substances to sniff. This may involve a pooling and sharing of
finances. On the other hand if the individual is without sufficient
money to buy his needs then other strategies will have to be adopted
which may involve solitary sniffers coming together and operating as a
group in order to steal items to sell or money to buy substances for
inhaling. Delinquent acts often associated with sniffing are house
breaking, burglary, shop lifting and handbag snatching. One group told
the author of how they would plan to steal tins of glue and dry cleaning
fluids from a supermarket or chain store. Three or four members of the
group would enter the store on the pretext of buying something but would
create a disturbance such as shouting and knocking over food displays to
distract the attention of the employees especially store detectives.
Meanwhile a lone member of the group could swiftly steal their supplies
and leave the shop unnoticed. There was also some talk of how older
pupils at school had bullied younger ones to give them money or to steal
tins of glue from shops for them.

   Another necessity in the case of glue sniffing is for a suitable
container from which to inhale. Most sniffers preferred to use plastic
bags. It is alleged that some shopkeepers actually gave a supply of
plastic freezer bags with each glue sale to teenagers. Sometimes large
plastic carrier bags were also used as part of the sniffing ritual in

which they were placed over the head and face and held open with the hands as the sniffer leaned over a tin of heated glue to capture as much of the vapour as possible.

Once the sniffer has selected a place and when he has all the supplies needed then the ritual of sniffing may begin. Making himself comfortable on the ground and sitting in a squatting position the contents of the volatile product can then be poured, sprayed or otherwise transferred to the plastic bag which thus primed is often referred to by terms such as, a charge, a charger or fix. Then expelling as much air from his lungs as possible the sniffer places the opening of the prepared bag to cover his mouth and nostrils and begins to breathe in and out rapidly for approximately 10 to 20 breaths, the average number seemed to vary between a dozen to 15 depending on the potency of the solution sniffed.

When the sniffer begins to experience the effects of intoxication he will sometimes pause to savour the pleasant mood changes and then resume sniffing until the real kicks commence such as feelings of acceleration and movement which eventually give way to numbness in which hallucinations figure largely. In the situation where a group were sniffing together there would usually be strange behaviours taking place when the group members started to feel high although the antics would differ with the individual concerned. Some sniffers talked a lot as if having conversations or arguments with some unseen person while others would rise and stagger about or dance. Even more bizarre were the screeching and rolling about fits of some sniffers. In some cases the sniffer would become extremely aggressive and begin to attack people and would have to be subdued by friends in the group. Mostly sniffers just sat around quietly enjoying the peaks and troughs of their own 'trips' as they called them. These latter if they did anything at all might be tattooing the self or another member on the hands or arms usually with some signs or words, such as a Nazi Swastike, a heart, cross or simply a series of darts as a badge signifying belonging to a particular skinhead or punk group. Common words found tattooed on sniffers attending the Clinic were: a girl's name, Mam or Mum; Dad; Hate; Filth; Pig; Fuck; Devil; etc. New members to special groups were required to be tattooed or mutilated with a particular sign or word as an initiation. Some sniffers said that they were told to sniff from a bag containing glue or some other volatile because the tatooing would not then be as painful. Here is an example of a punk group learning to apply these toxic gases to anaesthetise as well as to intoxicate in the same way as fun loving groups in the nineteenth century used nitrous oxide (Laughing gas).

In the usual course of a sniffer's day an individual might move from one location to several others either to sniff alone or to join a group or do a combination of both. Eating and drinking was generally done on the move and would ordinarily consist of a bag of chips or a meat pie supplemented by a chocolate bar or biscuits; to drink there would usually be tins of cola, or other fizzy drinks, sometimes it would be lager, cider or beer. One hundred and fifty sniffers attending the University Clinic were asked about their eating habits. Significantly 87 (49 boys, 38 girls) said they could not recall having a sit down meal at home during the last twelve months (58%). The picture which emerged was of a youngster eating as he walked from place to place or whilst standing.   The usual fare consumed was convenience foods which tended to be deficient in dietary supplements considered essential for the maintenance of good health.   Meeting up with friends or acquaintances at specific places or just following a familiar route alone and arriving at particular points along the way at approximately the same time each day provides the sniffer's daily life with a coherance which lends a sense of much needed security which is generally absent from other aspects of the individual's life.

For the chronic sniffer sleeping habits change radically and much time is spent awake during the hours of darkness.   Some sniffers said they were scared to sleep during the night because of the nightmares they had others said they liked to spend the night sniffing because it was quiet and nobody bothered them.   In the course of interviews with several hundred sniffers at the Clinic a picture developed of bedraggled and tired teenagers wending their way homewards with the dawn after a night of intoxicating satiation as if in mock imitation of the zombie and vampire figures which regularly filled their hallucinations.   For these sniffers the inhalation of volatile fumes becomes a routine which dominates their lives in a similar fashion to the ways in which hard drugs affect addicts.   Considered realistically in terms of the effects they have on the young people who inhale them, solvents and other volatile substances are cheap drugs which induce their own brand of addicition.   Sniffing becomes a substitute for ordinary living and imposes a fantasy reality on the sniffer who appears to live on a perpetual high of intoxication.   This alternative way of living, with its language, rituals and patterns of behaving as described above, assumes the dominant focus of the individual's conscious purpose in life to the virtual exclusion of all else.   It is not therefore surprising to find that nonsniffers among adolescents refer to the chronic sniffers as addicts and identify them with labels such as junkie borrowed from the hard drug scene, or since sniffing practices have become more widespread the derogatory term 'gluey' or 'glue sniffer' is applied with similar meaning.

Indications from the analyses of two samples of sniffers

Information on causation and motivation in sniffing practices was provided by two studies which were carried out on different populations in the North East of England.   The first sample consisted of a mixed population in care at an assessment and observation centre which comprised all admissions to the Centre during the months January to December 1980, and which numbered a total of 200 cases for each of which there were 25 items of information.   There were 28 identifiable cases of solvent abusers within this sample most of whom had been ordered into care because of problems associated with sniffing.   The information variables on which the cases were individually examined and compared within the overall group were:

date of birth	step mother	council house
solvent abuse	step father	private house
natural mother	remarried	position in family
natural father	mother working	family size
divorce	father working	offender

height	drinking alcohol excessively
weight	taking drugs
psychiatric disturbance of parents	violence
psychiatric disturbance	self mutilation
smoking	tattoos

This data was analysed to determine the degree of statistical relationship between the variables and solvent abuse. The results are illustrated in figure 4.1 from which it can be seen that the observed links between the items is tenuous as would be expected from the observed limitations for example: the small size of sample; bias towards a loading of young people suffering from the effect of family pathology; and the subjects belonged to a residential group in care as distinct from a normal school population. In spite of these limitations there are some interesting correlations to be observed which are possible indicators of meaningful links between variables to which sniffing activities may be attributed. The most significant result to emerge is the connection between marriage breakdown and solvent abuse. Such factors as the absence of mother or father from the family figured largely. These indications were especially noteworthy because of their similarity to noted information about cases attending the Clinic as may be seen from the results in figure 4.2.

Since the data is drawn from samples independent of each other it is interesting to observe that they both show broadly similar relationships between variables although it is necessary to caution against placing too much reliance on these results which at best are tentative. However, it is fair to say that the results are sufficiently promising to encourage further studies of this kind.

Accepting that any small scale study will have serious limitations as regards providing scientifically valid and reliable results it is nevertheless worth considering evidence from the case study angle. Researching the facts from individual case reports taken at the Clinic it is clear that regular quarrelling and fighting between parents leads to an atmosphere of tension and insecurity which unsettles young people in the family. A home environment made disorderly by parental mismanagement and neglect, where one of the parents has left to live elsewhere, where there is the unwelcome presence of a step mother or step father, are all factors with the potential of contributing to troublesome behaviour among adolescents, e.g. truancy, delinquency, running away from home, overdosing, glue sniffing and solvent abuse. But there is such a criss crossing of associations that it is a tortuous process trying to tease out the most significant causes for sniffing especially since the relative importance of the different elements will vary with the personality of the sniffer. It is vital to appreciate that close scrutiny of the individual case will tend to reveal the key factors involved although it has to be understood that the counsellor is often presented first of all with blocks and evasions when questioning about the motives for sniffing. The usual answer, 'Because I'm bored' will eventually lead to other more meaningful answers as the counselling relationship develops and all the background circumstances become known.

VOLATILE SUBSTANCE ABUSE IN A
RESIDENTIAL CARE POPULATION

The sample consisted of a mixed population in care at an assessment and
observation centre.   It comprised the total admissions over the period
January to December 1980.   There were 200 cases for each of which there
were 25 separate items of information (see pages 63 and 64 for further
details and list of variables).   Statistical analysis of the data was
carried out employing regression analysis and chi square but due
possibly to limiting factors already mentioned (see page 64) the results
did not indicate a high order of statistical significance.   The sub
sample of 28 sniffers amounted only to 14% of the sample overall.
There are however strong indications that some of the observed
relationships between the variables were meaningful in the context of
the subjective reports of the sniffers themselves and of the care staff
who worked with them.   Therefore the variables have been ranked in
order of degree of statistical relationship whilst accepting that only
the top factor showed significance for chi square at the 0.05 level.
The ranking for the first ten variables is given below to promote
comment and stimulate further studies.

Rank Order of Variables Inter-Correlating with sniffing.

1. Divorce.
2. Natural father absent (especially important in cases of
   girl sniffers).
3. Step mother.
4. Psychiatric disturbance of parent.
5. Tattoos.
6. Self mutilation.
7. Remarried.
8. Family size.
9. Council house.
10. Smoking.

N= 28 sniffers. 18 boys, 10 girls. Total sample N=200.

Average age for group of sniffers was 13.7 years with an age range of
13 to 17 years.

Figure 4.1

VOLATILE SUBSTANCE ABUSE AND RELATIONSHIPS
IN SNIFFERS ATTENDING A COUNSELLING CLINIC

Analysis of the cases attending for treatment at the Counselling Clinic was carried out with a view to evaluating the importance of certain variables in individual cases of sniffing. This analysis was three fold:

   a. From the person's own report during counselling.
   b. Reports from the parents when they attended clinic.
   c. Relevant items noted or subsequently learned by counsellors
      about individuals.

 On the basis of information derived from these cases the variables were ranked in order of importance and the first ten are listed below:

Rank Order of Variables Relating to Sniffing.

   1. Marital separation, disruption and divorce.
   2. Either mother or father missing from home through death or
      separation. Father absent seems more upsetting for girls
      but was also an important factor for boys.
   3. Presence of step mother or step father who was not loved.
   4. Family size. Too many children in family tended to have
      disruptive effects, (e.g. more than four children).
   5. Mother working.
   6. Self mutilation.
   7. Drinking alcohol excessively.
   8. Smoking.
   9. Offender.
   10.Overdosing,especially with girl sniffers.

Total number of cases attending counselling clinic on three occasions or more for treatment over the period September 1979 to March 1983 inclusive.

N= 529. Boys 343, girls 186.

Average ages, Boys 15.8 years, Girls 14.6 years.

Figure 4.2

5 MANAGEMENT

The management of adolescents with glue sniffing and solvent abuse problems is central to finding a solution overall. Many sniffers attending the Clinic present as being out of the control of their parents, teachers and other significant adults who share responsibilities for them. A father who brought his son aged 15 years to the Clinic said on his first visit: 'The wife and I just have to admit that Stephen is out of our control and we know other parents who feel the same way about their children'. Certainly the majority of parents attending the Clinic or those who telephoned the author asking for advice conveyed a sense of helplessness in relation to the misbehaviour of their offspring. For example over the period from January 1982 to April 1983 there were 86 parents who attended the Clinic either in the company of their children or alone. Of this number 73 (84.9%) confided that they felt unable to control the daughter or son who was presently being troublesome.

It is not helpful simply to apportion blame in these cases. The need is for planning which will break the cycle of parental incompetency perpetuated within some families from one generation to another with consequent deprivations for the children. Planning would entail providing guidelines on what is acceptable practice in functioning as a competent parent.

It is management provisions at this level which are important in combating problems arising through volatile substance abuse. Child management practices in the home so often depend for success upon genuine love and attention which is not solely indulgent but involves disciplining the self to behave in ways compatible with social and ethical standards. During the late 1950's and early sixties it became fashionable to rear children in a permissive way with the effect that parents were encouraged through the media to abdicate their traditional role of controlling and directing their children's behaviour. A study by Krug and Henry (1974) in the USA of adolescent drug use patterns which included glue sniffing, identified the lack of discipline and absence of trianing in societal or ethical standards in child rearing practices as being significant in adolescent drug abuse. At a more extreme level Skuse and Burrell (1982) in a survey of 45 solvent abusers referred to the child psychiatry department at Maudsley Hospital, London, found that most cases came from disrupted family backgrounds where the natural mothers were emotionally rejecting often from birth. It is not difficult to envisage the paucity of child management and training to which these children were exposed. In view of the importance of parental care as an effective management process to deal with sniffing both at the preventative and the remedial level, it is advisable to provide parents and those with professional responsibilities in child care with a set of guidelines. The form that these guidelines should most usefully take has been found to be a set of written instructions and advice which is given as a handout to parents requesting information on how to cope with a glue sniffer in the family. The following is the context of the handout which the author has used with success at the Clinic and which has been used by some social workers and teachers who were counselling parents of sniffers. It is reproduced verbatim here so that if necessary it may be used by the reader. The first section is written in a directly personal way to the parent in the form of an open letter to communicate the fullest possible sympathy for the parents' problems while at the same time giving guidance as to the most appropriate approach to adopt. The guidelines are the result of much discussion between the author and colleagues in the child caring professions especially those from health education.

GUIDELINES FOR PARENTS

It is probable that you felt shocked and upset when you learned that your child has been involved in sniffing and inhaling fumes from glues or some other substances. You will no doubt have been informed that sniffing is a fashionable activity among young people at the present time. For many youngsters sniffing can be a transient phase in which there is a certain amount of dabbling and experimenting which quickly passes. For some individuals, however, the practice becomes a habit which is not easy to stop. In these circumstances it is easy for parents to panic and over react because they are afraid of what might happen and feel let down by the thoughts of their son or daughter becoming intoxicated and acting in a drunken manner. However strongly you may feel it is preferable to show patience and resist the impulse to punish your child. Punishment does not seem to be effective in stopping the habit and physical punishment in the form of thrashing or smacking the youngster does not work, in fact it often makes matters worse by hurting the individual so badly that he or she starts sniffing again just to relieve these feelings. It is much better to wait until the effects of the sniffing have ceased and your child has completely recovered before engaging in any discussions about the activity. It is as well to try to understand that your child may have some personal reasons for sniffing such as being anxious about school, or worried about looking attractive or being accepted as a friend by others. Indeed it may be that there are reasons in the family which have contributed to your child becoming involved in sniffing. Whatever the reasons it is sensible to respond with kindness and acceptance whilst giving practical advice as this attitude promises the most hope of helping the young person to overcome the need to sniff. In this respect the following are useful hints to consider as to what is the most effective way to behave as a parent with the welfare of young people in mind.

Good Parenting

Young people desperately need to feel loved and secure. Good parents
will recognise such needs in their youngsters and take care to ensure
that their child or teenager feels loved to his or her satisfaction.
The following simple guidelines are steps which the anxious parent can
take to help a young person in trouble due to glue sniffing to work his
way back to normal.   For example parents should:

1. Take time to listen and talk to their youngsters without
    criticising or accusing or threatening.   This will help the
    young person to feel he can confide in his parents and rely
    upon their support in overcoming glue sniffing habits.

2. Show affection regularly by giving a hug or cuddle when
    appropriate to reassure the young person that they are really
    loved and wanted even although there are younger children
    about or especially if there has been a separation or divorce
    splitting the family.

3. Allow young people especially teenagers the freedom to express
    their own unique personalities without wanting to make them
    conform or to punish them for being different.

4. Take definite action to train young people to develop healthy
    activities such as sports, outdoor pursuits, hobbies and
    interests which will safeguard them against boredom and
    frustration, the two most commonly stated causes of glue
    sniffing behaviour.

5. Give a good example of how to enjoy life by showing healthy
    interests as above.   Parents might like to reflect seriously
    on the bad examples they can give their children by:

    excessive smoking and drinking of alcohol,
    taking pills and medicine regularly to feel good,
    over-emphasising sex at the expense of love and affection
      for each other.

    Such behaviour on the part of parents and the significant
    adults in a child or teenager's life can help to drive them
    to sniff glue or inhale solvents.

6. Above all try to be available in the home for your youngsters
    in the family at least 2 or 3 days during the week.   Try to
    spend more time with them, teenagers need the companionship
    of parents.   Relationships with father seem to be especially
    important judging from the way the young people talked about
    their needs at the Clinic.   Arrange to go places with them
    or to take them with you occasionally.   Take an interest in
    what they have been doing and where they have been without
    seeming judgemental or appearing as if you want to interfere.

Parents, especially mothers, have great influence for good, and with
patience, affection and toleration any young person can be helped to
overcome serious problems such as glue sniffing and solvent abuse.

69

The following case is an example which makes this point very well.

Mrs. Donohue is mother to three boys and two girls. Her husband is a prematurely retired miner who suffered an accident in the pits which left him partially disabled. Two years ago Mrs. Donohue discovered that her eldest son Terry was glue sniffing to a chronic level. He would come into the house in a highly inebriated state each night often collapsing in one of the downstairs rooms where he would spend the rest of the night. Mrs. Donohue was afraid that he would suffer an accident during his inebriated state and she would lie awake listening for him coming into the house. During the night she would usually check that he was sleeping on his side, not his back, so that if he vomited he would not choke to death. Sometimes she left the house to search for him. Once she discovered him lying in the roadway where he'd fallen and cut his head. The strain on Mrs. Donohue's health became so intense that she fell ill. Her weight fell by two stones to 7½ stones but she persisted in looking after her son treating him with loving care and devotion until the time came when he realised the extent of his predicament and volunteered to come to the Clinic for treatment. Eventually he succeeded in overcoming his dependency and admitted that he owed his recovery chiefly to his mother whose selfless care and faith had at last succeeded in giving him new hope in his own life. 'I owe her everything', he said. 'She even accompanied me, a 19 year old to the Clinic each week when she should have been in bed herself. She saved my life. If she'd given up on me I would have been finished'.

HOW TO HELP THE SNIFFER TO MANAGE HIS DEPENDENCY

Glue sniffing and solvent inhalation can be much more difficult to stop than young people realise. Those who desire to give up usually need help to succeed especially if they have been sniffing over a long period of time. The worst cases often need prolonged treatment to overcome dependency on solvent fumes.

The first step towards helping the youngster to manage himself is to identify and talk about the problem from the sniffers' point of view. To talk out the feelings he or she has about sniffing and above all listen to what the sniffers have to say. The problem can only be dealt with effectively if the person concerned sees sniffing as a problem. Attention needs to be given therefore to how the person feels he is suffering. Young people experience the ill effects of solvent sniffing differently. Some youngsters are more aware of the physical symptoms of poisoning from solvents. Others wish to stop because they realise that their behaviour is causing distress to others especially family and friends. Some find that they have committed offences against the law whilst intoxicated and now have to face the consequences. But a great many sniffers find that living in a dream world of hallucinations is not so good after all and they just want to get back to normal. It is important that treatment starts with whatever reason the sniffer gives for wanting to stop. The best way to help is to listen and give support without being critical or angry. Friendly acceptance together with understanding for the young person's feelings will do much towards finding a solution to the problem. Trying to frighten the sniffer by listing the possible ill effects is usually not as worthwhile as urging the young person to say why he thinks he should stop.

This way encourages the youngster to think for himself and avoids a
stubborn refusal against being told what to do by parents or those in
authority like teachers and policemen. The important message to get
over to all concerned is that with patience and kindness young people
can succeed in overcoming the need for glue and other solvent fumes.

Once a youngster has made up his own mind to stop then he can be
helped by following these simple guidelines:

Find out when sniffing is most likely to happen and where. Plan to do
something interesting and healthy instead, such as: taking part in
sports, joining a youth club, finding a hobby, read exciting books to
get dreams and fantasies. Keep away from groups of sniffers. Avoid
places where sniffers go.

To relieve ill effects of sniffing try: breathing exercises twice a day,
eat plenty of fresh fruit especially oranges (vitamin C helps the body
to rid itself of poisons). Drink a full glass of water morning and
night to clean out the kidneys. Eat raw onions and garlic to help the
lungs to recover. Arrange to have a properly cooked sit down meal once
a day with plenty of proteins and fresh vegetables. Consult a doctor
if painful and worrying symptoms persist. Above all ask for help to
stop sniffing. It's not a good idea to drink alcohol or smoke tobacco
instead of sniffing. These activities can be just as dangerous in the
long term and can themselves lead to addiction.

MULTI DISCIPLINARY APPROACHES TO MANAGING THE GLUE SNIFFER

In April 1982 Strathclyde Regional Council issued a document entitled
'Solvent Abuse, A Corporate Approach' which represented the efforts of
many professional groups in child care and welfare to achieve a
co-ordinated approach to the problems arising from solvent abuse.
Sniffing volatiles has a long history in Scotland dating back to the
beginning of the seventies. Dr. Joyce Watson has pioneered an almost
single handed approach to the problem on the West Coast of Scotland and
it is largely due to her research efforts that the authorities in the
Strathclyde area have become so aware of the need for a multi
disciplinary approach which seeks to integrate the previously frag-
mented professional responses to these abuses. The guidelines
recommended by the Report are essentially practical in suggesting how
the problem can be tackled in a unified manner by co-ordinating the
services of the police, social work, education and the different
agencies for juvenile care including the health boards and the
Reporter's Department.

The management strategy proposed by this Report is that a meeting
should be called by the Divisional Director of Social Work involving
representatives of all the caring agencies in the locality where
solvent abuse is a problem. These agencies should be advised to set up
local corporate groups to deal with the specifics of the problem and one
of the agencies should be nominated as the co-ordinating agency and its
representative become the co-ordinator of local strategy on the problem.
The function of this organisation should be to co-ordinate an integrated
response to the problem by ensuring that incidents of solvent abuse

receive appropriate attention and intervention. A pleasing feature of the strategies to be employed is that they are aimed at prevention as well as dealing with crises. For example, there are details of hand-outs to be circulated in the area alerting shopkeepers to the dangers of selling products containing solvents and other volatiles to young folk, and there are various guidelines on the most suitable ways of responding to chronic cases of sniffing which could be issued to appropriate agencies and individuals.

The real worth of the management plan is that people, the lay public and professionals, are informed in detail of what to do if and when the problem of sniffing is encountered whether it is by a teacher, social worker, policeman, or parent. The information provided is basic and is intended to give the caring adult knowledge of the problem and clear directions on how to proceed. The following sub-headings will indicate the detailed nature of the planned management strategy:

    Notes for school staff,
    Main hazards to sniffers,
    Identification of solvent abuser,
    What to watch for,
    Action you should take.

The information given under the above headings is also intended to prepare people to be able to respond positively to the incidents of sniffing they encounter rather than giving way to alarm and panic which might lead to rejection of the need for action of any kind on the assumption that if we pretend that there is no problem it will cease to exist. From a preventative viewpoint the best method is to adopt a school based health education programme which does not unduly emphasise the topic of glue sniffing but attempts to deal with it as a part of a general programme on drug and alcohol education. As far as possible the pupils should be encouraged to do project work where they can gather the facts for themselves on sniffing. This approach is preferable to the potentially challenging method of having an 'expert' address the pupils en masse on the dangers of sniffing which could easily invite more sniffing through experimentation.

Ian Peers (1983) wrote a Report entitled 'Solvent Abuse; Educational Implications' for the Teachers Advisory Council on Alcohol and Drug Education (TACADE) in which there is much sound advice on the management of the problem. Taken from the Report the following suggestions are the types of action the school could take when faced with the problem of glue sniffing among pupils:

1. The school should seek support and co-operation from parents and community.

2. The school should undertake its own preventative programme.

3. In terms of treatment for solvent abuse the school should refer the 'problem children' to the appropriate support agencies, e.g. school psychological services or social services and suitable supervision procedures may have to be developed.

It is further suggested that any work within the curriculum on solvent abuse should be integrated within a combined programme of health, social and personal education. Trial material for suggested lessons is included as a guide for the teacher with the strong provision that the objectives stated in this material are and should always be pupils' objectives. The implications of the Report which it seems are becoming increasingly accepted as a responsible educational approach to pupils sniffing problems is to adopt a long term strategy which is aimed at the person rather than the sniffing behaviour. Examples of projects which incorporate the development of both good health and personal growth are the following:

5-13 Schools Council Health Education Project.
The Careers Research Advisory Centre (CRAC) publications on decision making.
The Lancashire Curriculum Development Teams' Active Tutorial Work Project which includes social skills training.
TACADE's set of 20 stimulation cards, called 'Understanding Others'.

In combination with projects such as the above it is also recommended that structured discussion groups should be set up as part of an education for personal relationships programme. Such a group would be involved in discussing adolescent problems in general and would only refer to sniffing problems if they were mentioned by the pupils.

In consideration overall of the need for management strategies to contain and control the problems arising from volatile substance abuses it is important to bear in mind that to achieve effective outcomes a realistic approach will have to be adopted in which existing agencies are employed to provide the necessary care. As Mike Ashton (1983) states in Drug Link there is an emerging picture of chronic solvent abuse as part of a syndrome of emotional disturbance and solvent misuse in general which is just one feature of adolescent delinquent behaviour. The practical implications are that existing services such as child psychiatry units and other general services for disturbed children should be mobilised to take the responsibility of caring for the sniffers.

A useful publication in this connection with which the writer was actively concerned is a pamphlet called 'Solvent Vapour Inhalation (Glue Sniffing), Notes for Professionals in Child Care', which was produced by the Drug Liaison Group at the Health Education Centre of Newcastle upon Tyne Area Health Authority (Teaching). This pamphlet like many similar ones produced throughout the country is intended to inform those who have a professional responsibility for adolescents about problems related to solvent abuses and to direct them where to make referrals for treatment. These small documents produced most often by health education authorities serve an extremely useful purpose in directing attention of the professional welfare services to managing by themselves the problems arising from chronic sniffing activities without feeling the need for new treatment centres to be set up. In this connection it was realised at a very early stage of collecting data on the cases attending the University Counselling Clinic that behind the presenting symptoms of glue sniffing there lay a familiar

profile of emotional upset and deprivation about which there was
nothing new.   It follows therefore that professionals involved in care
work are already trained to cope with these problems.   Indeed the
Corporate Approach mentioned at the beginning of this section is an
illustration of how the existing care services can be employed to manage
and initiate treatment for the sniffers without needing much in the way
of additional resources.

6 TREATMENT

The increasing incidence of problems which are referred to professional caring services arising through the deliberate inhalation of solvent vapours by young people has intensified the search for effective remedies.   But these problems are not easy to solve.   Jamieson (1980) puts it aptly when he writes: 'To ask for a cure for glue sniffing is like asking for a cure for delinquency'.   Accepting that there can be no easy cure for the habitual abuse of volatile substances means that if any treatment is to prove effective in the long term then therapeutic attention will need to be directed at least as much towards the personality of the sniffer as to the symptoms of sniffing behaviour. The best results from therapy will only be achieved if changes in behaviour are accompanied by a change of attitude by the person indulging these intoxicants.   Further it would appear that the inhalation of solvent vapours and the attendant troubles constitute for many young people a fashionable way of presenting a need for therapy which derives from underlying problems.   It is essential therefore that each patient presenting with solvent abuse problems be considered as an individual and that his own personal needs be fully explored.   It is necessary throughout the caring relationship for the therapist to main-tain an eclectic view of all forms of treatment available so that these may be applied or adapted especially to meet the needs of the individual case.

   Treatment for sniffers has largely been neglected except in cases of extreme physical emergency or nervous breakdown which is surprising in view of the research evidence already accumulated on other forms of drug abuse.   In considering the most appropriate approaches to treatment for sniffers it is worthwhile reviewing the evidence on adolescent drug abuse.   To understand the factors operating in adolescent drug abuse it is necessary to consider how the drug functions for the user.   Drugs serve different functions for the same person at different times. Following Cross and Kleinhesselink (1980) the various circumstances governing drug use are briefly described below with obvious applications to sniffing abuses.

   Experimentation: drugs are used to have fun, explore how feelings
                     change under their influence and to satisfy
                     curiosity.

Social interactional: Drugs are used to share common experiences and commune with friends.

Circumstantial and Situational: Drugs are used to help in coping with moods, feelings about work and sex.

Intensified: Drugs are used to escape from problems including emotional problems and bad memories.

Compulsive: Drugs are used to maintain an intoxicated high feeling, a drugged state.

It follows that since the use of drugs can take various forms and serve different functions it is restrictive to view drugs simply in terms of use or non use. Most adolescents will experiment with drugs if only with so-called legal drugs such as cigarettes, alcohol, pain killers, sedatives and tranquilisers (benzodiazephines). Sharing alcohol, coffee and cigarettes is a common practice among adolescents and adults and illustrates the strong cultural forces at work which encourage people to take drugs. This fact has to be understood when considering what will be the most effective approaches to the prevention and treatment of illicit drug use. For the teenage abuser this attitude of society towards drug usage can often appear ambivalent with some justification. Except for those drugs which are forbidden by law, drug use is considered to be a problem only when drugs are used to escape from reality rather than simply to help the person with daily activities. Chronic glue sniffing and the abuse of solvents and volatiles falls mainly into this category but it has to be recognised that sniffers are often abusing other drugs as well as volatiles notably alcohol. This needs to be taken into account when treatment programmes are initiated since the taking of one drug may well trigger taking others and drug counsellors can find themselves faced with a series of abuses rather than the relative simplicity of a lone glue sniffing problem. In broad terms it is necessary to examine the extent to which environmental influences teach the young person that drug taking is an OK experience which everyone accepts. If treatment strategies are to do more than shift patterns of drug use from illicit to licit forms it is vital to consider the totality of the person's drug taking behaviour. Since the substances which are inhaled in sniffing abuses are not illegal the problems facing the therapist from VSA are compounded even more.

In relation to the above it can be seen that the individual's attitude to sniffing as well as the pattern his sniffing behaviour takes are important issues from the treatment angle. It is important therefore to inquire as carefully as possible into the way the person perceives his own sniffing activities. In this connection a leaflet produced by Alcoholics Anonymous entitled 'A Message to Teenagers' sets out a number of questions the answers to which can help the drinker to know when drinking becomes a problem. These questions have been adapted to provide a similar service for the sniffer who is prepared to answer them truthfully and are listed below:

Do you sniff because you have problems?
When you are alone?
When you get mad?

Are you skiving off work?
Do you sniff in the morning before school or work?
Do you suffer loss of memory due to sniffing?
Do you get really high even when you don't want to?
Do you feel big to be able to sniff and get high?
Do you get low marks at school?
Do you ever try to sniff less or stop and fail?
Do you sniff a lot quickly because you are craving for it?
Do you tell lies about how much you sniff?

Answers to questions such as these can help the counsellor to understand the individual's reasons for sniffing and how best to help him.
It remains a sad fact however that unless the sniffer is motivated
enough to want to stop then the chances of achieving effective treatment
outcomes are very remote.   Such a series of questions might help the
sniffer to become aware that he has a problem and therefore of the need
to seek help.

Cases of glue sniffing and solvent abuse among the adolescent school
and post school populations are referred through a variety of social and
educational caring agencies to a Voluntary Counselling Clinic at the
University of Newcastle upon Tyne, School of Education referred to
earlier in this text.   Some cases are self referred others are sent or
accompanied by parents, social workers, probation officers, youth
workers, teachers, general practitioners and some are recommended
through the juvenile courts.

At the initial treatment sessions the approach usually applied is
one-to-one client centred, non directive psychotherapy as a means of
achieving an effective rapport with the patient and towards obtaining
essential autobiographical data.   At a later stage a treatment policy
incorporating, for instance, a behaviour modification programme, or
confrontation technique deriving from Gestalt psychotherapy may be
adopted according to the therapist's assessment of the form of
counselling needed by the patient.

The Counselling Clinic

The Clinic is housed in a converted terraced house of Georgian design
owned by the University of Newcastle upon Tyne.   At these premises
mature students drawn from teaching, social work and residential care
are reading for advanced qualifications in Counselling Psychology.   As
part of their practical studies in developing caring skills they are
required to counsel young people with problems.

The Clinic opens at 10.30 each Saturday morning and usually closes
when there are no more clients that day, at approximately 4.30 to 5.00
p.m.   Referrals, including self-referrals, are accepted from anywhere
in the region;   where possible, appointments are made but no one is
turned away.   Parents often turn up with their teenage son or daughter
and very often they need counselling as well.   Social workers, teachers
probation officers, youth workers and police from the community welfare
branch are among the professionals who send young people to the Clinic
and who sometimes actually accompany a teenager on a first visit.

On arrival a new client is shown to a reception area where he can sit in a relaxed atmosphere and have a cup of tea or coffee in the company of other clients. Within this group there are at least two counsellors who work hard at creating a receptive client centred atmosphere. Also in the group will be a few individuals who have been successfully weaned from their dependence on solvents and who are now able to help others through peer counselling, since teenagers are more likely to identify positively with each other than with adults. Each client is seen individually for counselling and a further appointment is made for the following week. When a client has been attending the clinic for several weeks and it is considered opportune, he will be asked to join others for group counselling. The atmosphere is engineered to be as informal as possible in order to reduce stress for the client. As one 15 year old summed up his first impressions:

'I didn't really want to come. But things were getting so bad I was ready to try anything to stop. I expected to be criticised and preached at but everybody was so nice to me that I couldn't believe it. I knew then if I kept coming I might be able to stop glue sniffing.'

The absence of any compulsion to attend helps to convey the message that clients need to make up their minds to help themselves in partnership with the counsellors who are guiding them. Whilst the primary function of the clinic is to provide a counselling service for young people troubled by solvent inhalation and abuses, it also has the purpose of gathering research data which will improve knowledge in this area.

THE EFFECTIVENESS OF PSYCHOLOGICAL APPROACHES

It is possible to evaluate the different psychological approaches to treatment for cases of volatile substance abuse (VSA) by referring both to the particular method used and the outcomes in terms of the behaviour and the feelings of the sniffers. Evidence drawn from clinical studies for example Krasowski (1979) and O'Connor (1981) appears to indicate that there are features of VSA cases which appear similar to psychological conditions supposedly operating in many cases of drug abuse such as a need to reduce stress and intolerable inferiority feelings. Methods of treatment for VSA cases which respond to these psychogenic factors should predictably therefore offer more favourable outcomes than dealing exclusively with the ill effects as a medical or pharmacological problem.

In searching for effective methods of treatment for VSA it is essential to investigate the psychological background of the patient whose VSA practices are more than likely just one manifestation of a much greater personality problem. Young people who habitually abuse volatile substances tend to present as immature, inadequate and insecure. As the young person grows through the formative adolescent period he is often not self confident enough to cope with frequent challenges to his concept of self and may seek a less threatening style of life within a glue sniffing and solvent abuse sub culture where he can more easily gain relief from anxiety. Since the original function of the abuse was to erect a defence between the individual and his personal difficulties both of these factors have to be considered if any treatment is to be effective. That is the intoxicating practice must be terminated and the patient needs to be helped to live happily without it. It is considered that therapeutic procedures to be adopted with the cases of VSA will rarely prove successful if a single treatment style is used mainly because of complications presented by VSA such as:

a. The difficulty of achieving any supervisory control of the patient's behaviour which is for example possible with drug abuse where residential hospital detoxification units are available.

b. VSA intoxication practices are not illegal so that there are no statutory sanctions as with some drug abuses, which can be applied as pressure to persuade sniffers to receive treatment.

Even when a patient expresses willingness to co-operate with treatment offered there are so many factors to be managed and controlled that a multi strategy approach is envisaged as having most prospect of success. In view of this it is essential to incorporate methods of management alongside treatment in attempting therapeutic approaches to Volatile Substance Abuse (VSA). That is to enlist the aid of parents, professional services, voluntary organisations like the churches Samaritans and the peer group in order that the personal counselling will have most chance of success.

Psychological Approaches to Treatment –
some initial considerations

Any psychological approach to treatment of VSA needs to carefully consider if not necessarily respond to the subjective state of the individual. One of the most important features which requires consideration from a treatment point of view is the question of the extent to which VSA cases develop dependency on the chemical vapours they inhale. Psychotherapy will be aimed at dealing with the under-lying mechanisms involved but the presence of withdrawal symptoms in many cases of long term sniffing as mentioned earlier in the text suggests that there may well be a requirement for detoxification to enable psychological treatment to become effective. Human dependency on chemicals which alter conscious states is a complex phenomenon which merits more attention than can be given here. There are however some interesting points which arise and which deserve research scrutiny such as: Is it useful to try to distinguish, as some studies do, (ISDD, 1980) between psychological and physiological dependency in acute cases of VSA? It could possibly be the case that dependency on VSA can perhaps best be represented by the example of a continuum which, at one extreme consists of subjective states which are described in psychological dependency terms of needs, wants and cravings, for the feelings associated with intoxication from volatiles (Watson, 1982), and at the other extreme consists of physiological states of dependency which can best be described in terms of neuro pharmacological reactions of body cells to certain chemicals which disorganise their function (Clark and Tinston, 1982). Another factor which appears to be related to dependency is the tolerance levels which

develop in cases of long term VSA e.g. 6-12 month sniffing period.
Watson (1979) reports one case which showed signs consistent with
physical withdrawal symptoms and comments further that all cases of
chronic VSA appeared to require external help to stop the habit.

Sniffers attending the Clinic for treatment expect help for their
problems as they see them.   It is common for them to voice anxieties
for treatment which will alleviate painful symptoms (see fig.3.1)
which recurr after a sniffing session.   It is not unusual for
counsellors to be asked for a pill to take away the ill effects and to
allow sniffing excesses to proceed without harm so unrealistic and
naive are some of the sniffers encountered at the Clinic.   The cri de
coeur is plainly saying, 'I am too weak to help myself please do it for
me.   Make it so that I don't need to sniff any more'.   Family, friends
interested professionals such as social workers, probation officers and
teachers also have expectations of treatment which emphasise the need
for action to stop the sniffing which they tend to feel cannot be
accomplished alone.   It seems to be the consensus of opinion, both
professional and lay, that the best approach to treatment is through a
team of caring people working towards a shared aim.   In the pages
which follow there are descriptions of techniques employed at the Clinic
to help sniffers and it is not always mentioned that the counsellors
rely heavily on the support when they can get it from parents and
professionals to support and sustain their weekly treatment efforts
throughout each day of the week.   Let it be understood that this
support in promoting effective outcomes with sniffers is highly valued
at the Clinic and without it the Clinic's capability for success in
treating sniffers would be markedly reduced.

Treatments

The deciding factors in choice of the treatment techniques to be
employed in an individual case is often how the person presents his
problem to the therapist.   In this respect attention is carefully
directed to the non verbal aspects of behaviour as providing a more
reliable indication than words alone to the individual's state of mind,
with regard, for instance, to the following key areas:

a.   Whether the individual sincerely wishes to end this abuse
     or is simply complying with pressures to make him appear
     as if he does.

b.   The degree of stress he is suffering as a result of the
     symptoms generated by solvent abuse.

c.   The significance of the ill effects of solvent abuse on
     the quality of life for the person at, 1. The Physiological
     level, 2. The level of family and social relationships.
     3. The psychological level.

This information is necessary to help the counsellor to begin to work
towards a close rapport with the sniffer to the point where particular
methods of counselling can be employed as therapies for the individual's
problems.   Whatever the special method of treatment emerges from the
counselling relationship it is evident that the underlying feature of
the therapy, whatever the form may be, is suggestion.   Suggestion as

80

an important part of the therapeutic process can take various forms, for example:

1. The implied suggestion that the individual is capable of healing himself and will do so under the care of the therapist.

2. The suggestion, reinforced by the individual's subsequent experience, that if a particular course of guidance is followed then matters will improve to a satisfactory outcome.

3. The suggestion that if the person can work through, in the present some traumatic experiences that have served to burden his life in the past, he will feel better.

It is essential for the therapist to understand the power of suggestion in the counselling relationship with 'glue sniffers'. The under-mentioned points are worthy of note in this respect:

1. One of the effects of long term chronic solvent inhalation and abuse is that progressive intoxication of the central nervous system by these chemicals affects the psychological condition to the point where the discriminative sense is impaired.

2. As the ability to perceive the environment realistically is lowered so the individual's susceptibility to suggestion is heightened, a development following severe intoxication during which the patient suffers hallucinations of a particularly vivid kind.

3. Because of the experience of 1 and 2 above the individual's initial excitement gives way to confusion and fear at the occurrence of mental phenomena which are beyond his control and which cause him to seek help.

Following the development of a counselling relationship with the person then a particular treatment style will be adopted. The following is a description of some of the methods of counselling employed with sniffers at the Clinic beginning with the person centred approach elements of which are basic to many other therapies.

The Person Centred Approach

The method of client centred non directive psychotherapy developed by Carl Rogers in the USA (Rogers, 1952), has contributed significantly to counselling practice in the UK. Fundamentally the method employs an attention centred technique aimed at creating a warm, genuine and empathic relationship in which the patient experiences unconditional acceptance. The affect is to facilitate the discharge of stressed emotions for the patient* leading to the emergence of a more balanced

*With special reference to this section on treatments it was considered to be more appropriate to use the term patient instead of client to indicate the suffering and need for care of individuals presenting at the Clinic for help.

and less threatened self which is the eventual objective of therapy. For young persons indulging VSA the method serves to establish a close rapport which often results in a speedy reduction of the negative feelings which tend to motivate sniffing activities. The chief disadvantage of the method is that for full effectiveness the counselling has to be of long term duration and relies heavily on the individual's developing insight into his own problems through articulating these sufficiently to cause remission of the undesired behaviour. The main advantage of a person centred approach to cases of VSA is that it establishes a firm basis for effective management of the problem since it tends to allay the anxiety and fears of patients about treatment and opens the way to the introduction of other more directive methods. The outcome of this approach to counselling sniffers seems to be in practice that it helps patients to relax sufficiently to benefit from more specific and short term treatments. It also has useful applications to family therapy.

The importance of the person centred approach from the subjective point of view of the patient is that the method creates an atmosphere of warmth and relaxation in which the individual experiences possibly for the first time, a non threatening relationship with an adult. The therapeutic value of this for the person is enormous judging by the comments of young people afterwards when they have overcome their sniffing habits and return to the Clinic to renew friendly contacts.

Whilst it is hard to identify those factors which are most instru- mental in causing sniffing behaviour it is still possible to indicate vital needs which if unsatisfied will lead the person to search for substitute satisfactions which may take the form of intoxication through alcohol, volatile substances or other drugs. A particular case reference will illustrate the nature of these vital needs:

Michael belongs to a punk group near his home in Washington, Tyne and Wear. On his first visit to the Clinic he presented a fearsome spectacle. He was dressed in black knee high boots with high heels, tight black jeans fastened by a thick belt with a large brass buckle. Over his bare chest he wore a thin open black leather waistcoat heavily studded and a huge ornate pendant hung from a chain around his neck. His arms were bare except for wrist bands which were also thickly covered with studs. He had pins and small studs through both ears and one in the left side of his nose. Both cheeks were marked with self inflicted tattoos as were the upper parts of his arms and chest. His hair was styled into two striking mohican type displays which were multicoloured red, green and yellow.

Michael's presenting problem was that he could not get an erection and did the Clinic provide pills to help with this condition. The author who was counselling Michael, felt that this boy was desperately trying to appear older than his seventeen years and that his problem was aimed at creating an impression of adulthood. It later transpired as he began to talk about himself that sex was the least of his problems. In the normal course of the counselling he was questioned about the quality of his relationships within the family and with friends. He became very reticent at this line of inquiry and looked most uncomfortable. Eventually he was asked a question which often yields a meaningful response in the clinical setting. He was asked: 'Is there anyone in your family who gives you a cuddle? Is there anyone in your family whom you can cuddle?' He answered by lowering his head and beginning to weep.

It was at this stage that the vivid presenting display began to fade and the emotionally fraught little boy began to emerge within the warmth empathy, and genuineness created by the Rogerian type counselling relationship. From that moment onwards he was more open about his feelings and the counselling really began to progress towards working things out for him.

As the above example shows there are some adolescent personalities who so desperately need to make up for a lack of loving care and attention in their lives that intoxicating drugs are used to give comfort and to soothe feelings of loneliness. Solvents and volatiles are undoubtedly used to fill these emotional gaps for some young people. The evidence from chronic cases attenting the Clinic shows strong indications that absence of loving touch contact with the family circle, e.g. cuddles, hand holding, hugs, kisses between parents and offspring at the adolescent stage, appear to be a significant factor contributing to the VSA behaviour. Broadly similar findings have been reported by Masterton (1979) in relation to alcohol abuse.

Further to the above points the most experienced counsellors at the Clinic were asked individually to identify the elements in their counselling which they believed were most conducive to effective outcomes with sniffers. The answers of each of the twelve counsellors asked were unanimous in identifying 'Attentive listening' as being the most important skill in the counselling relationship. As a balance a small sample of 98 patients who had over six month period June to December 1982 attended for five or more treatment sessions at the Clinic were asked what it was about the Clinic that had helped them the most. The answers fell into four simple groups which are listed below:

Patient reply categories and distribution   %

Being able to talk to someone who would listen	63	64.30
Getting advice on how to stop sniffing	18	18.36
Learning to relax	13	13.26
Being cured	4	4.08
N=98 Total	98	100.00

As can be seen from the above it is evident that the experience of having someone actually spend time in listening to a person talking about how it feels to be involved in sniffing is very therapeutic both from the patient's and the counsellor's point of view. The replies listed in the table above were grouped according to the first replies given. When the remaining 35% who did not answer according to the first grouping were asked directly if they found the experience of talking to a counsellor in a one to one situation helpful they all agreed that it had been. The value of this exercise is to highlight the fundamental worth of the person centred techniques where listening and attention giving in a one to one counselling situation may be all that is happening. It seems that this alone is sufficient to set in motion the process of behaviour change.

Whenever possible the parents of sniffers are contacted with a view to attending the Clinic for discussions about how they might contribute to the management and treatment of the problem. Sometimes it is the mother or father who first contacts the Clinic for help and guidance. In these cases of family counselling it is often more useful to hear the feelings of each individual preferably when together with a view to developing more tolerant, accepting, loving and yet disciplined family relationship aimed at supporting the young person in learning to cope with his problems. The method of client centred psychotherapy is considered to be essential to creating the right foundations for family counselling to proceed effectively with VSA so that relationships which are at risk, through for example: feelings of jealousy by sniffers towards other siblings, lack of loving care contact and dialogue between sniffer and parents especially father, may be worked through satisfact- orily in an atmosphere of acceptance and calm with a counsellor present to facilitate the treatment process. Small family group counselling of this kind is probably the most rewarding from the counsellor's point of view because the hoped for results appear to be immediately discernible since everybody is seen to be heard and acknowledged to have a point of view. On one occasion the author had brought together a family of four, mother, father and teenage brother and sister. This family it seems rarely met each other except in passing. Mother was going out to work in an office when father was returning home from nightshift in a local factory. Brother and sister, 14 and 15 years respectively, were usually at loggerheads and not on speaking terms. They had not been together very long before they began to really talk to each other and start to share their individual experiences. They got on so well together that the counsellor was able to leave them together alone and it was over an hour before they left. Not only that but they came regularly over the next six weeks namely to meet up with and talk to each other on the neutral ground of the Clinic although in addition the boy and the girl also received individual counselling.

As this example is meant to illustrate it would be hard for the author to overestimate the value in practice of the client centred method. It has proved so valuable at the Clinic and so simple to apply that even trainee counsellors quickly learn to use the method effectively.

Behavioural Approaches

In many cases of VSA it is useful to employ methods of behaviour modification (McMaster, 1982) as a method of counselling which moves the emphasis away from the symptoms identified through the use of assessment labels such as glue sniffer and solvent abuser towards those mani- festations of behaviour which are dangerous and troublesome and which seem to occur as a result of VSA, for example: aggressive behaviour in the home and fighting with the family, violence and vandalism to people and property within the community such as frightening old people living in tower flats and wrecking telephones and lifts; sniffing alone and using a fire to heat glue to increase vaporisation; placing a large plastic carrier bag over the head to trap the vapour from the substance; etc. The focus of therapeutic attention in behavioural approaches to VSA is the interaction of the sniffer with the environment. Barnes in his review of solvent abuse (Barnes, 1979) reflects on the evidence that prevalence of sniffing is linked with learned helplessness due to adverse environmental conditions. He comments further that when people are faced with situations which they cannot change for the better they will often attempt to improve their psychological state pharmacologically.

The important connections here for behaviour therapy is that learned helplessness can be changed by social and life skills training which teaches the individual how to develop coping strategies to offset adverse environmental conditions and disabling states of anxiety. New ways of behaving towards problem situations can be learned by first of all directing the sniffer's awareness to the wide range of alternative activities which are given to him. For example: sporting and leisure activities. From their own accounts it appeared that many of the young people attending the Clinic had never experienced playing games for fun partly it seemed due to living in a deprived environment accentuated by parental neglect and partly because over zealous teachers enforced game playing as part of the school curriculum and caused inhibitions to set in. The need here is for such individuals to be introduced to games and sporting activities for pleasure which would tend to reinforce more positive outgoing behaviour to offset the withdrawal type behaviour of VSA. In all of this the young people appreciate helpful guidance but resist being pushed into and forced to do things. The field study centre visit has been used very successfully by many schools.

Similarly many cases of VSA are found to be deficient on examination at the Clinic in reading skills. It seems that in these cases word identification has been learned but has not developed to the fluency of reading which enables the reader to enjoy the mental images which accompany the written word. To teach these individuals to read fluently can be most helpful in weaning them away from VSA since for many sniffers it is the hallucinations which they find so rewarding and which therefore tend to reinforce the habit. Reading stories serves to present the sniffer with alternative forms of escaping into phantasy without the painful after effects of VSA. The ego boosting experience for the non reader of finding a whole new world opening up for him can produce remarkable remissions of behaviour problems including sniffing activities.

In addition to the above there are other counselling approaches to changing the behaviour of sniffers which have contributed to successful treatment outcomes at the Clinic. For example: the tendency for patients to identify with the counsellors and to begin to model themselves accordingly. Related to this is the degree to which some of the patients respond to the peer counselling of the ex-patients who have been successfully treated and return to help out at the Clinic. In such cases the modelling seems to occur as part of the natural process of identifying with other teenagers who present attractively because they have overcome dependency on VSA. Afterall it seems that since peer group pressure is a major factor in promoting VSA it is useful to employ these pressures to helping sniffers to copy young people who have successfully weaned themselves from VSA.

A more precise behavioural approach is to chart a day by day account of the sniffer's behaviour during the week and to concentrate attention on the times when the desired behaviour occurs, e.g. activities which

do not involve sniffing.   The power of the counsellor's behaviour in
the relationship to reward the patient's 'good behaviour' by non verbal
signs of approval such as smiles, head nods, congratulatory touch and
gestures, as well as verbal support, should not be underestimated since
it constitutes an effective means of reinforcing non sniffing behaviour.
Sometimes it is appropriate to draw up contracts in which the sniffers
undertake to accept responsibility for controlling a part of their own
behaviour during the week and in some cases tangible rewards such as
chocolate bars, or a day's outing, e.g. on a fishing trip with a
counsellor, are given to reward successful behaviour in the early stages
of therapy to accelerate improvement and to give the sniffer a good
feeling of having achieved something positive.   Additionally advice on
diet and exercise can serve to further direct attention towards
behavioural changes.

A related form of behavioural counselling which is increasingly
popular at the present time is the use of Video Tape Recording apparatus
(VTR).   This approach has been used successfully to counsel cases of
drug addiction in the USA, (Berger, 1978) and has achieved wide usage in
behavioural approaches known as micro training.   As a counselling tool
VTR is basically a means of directing the patient's attention towards
his general non verbal behaviour, e.g. appearance, movements, posture
and gestures.   The benefit of VTR is that the patient can view his own
behaviour on the television monitor more dispassionately than the more
personal confrontation of having a counsellor describe it to him and
becomes therefore self directed to seek change.   In this way cases of
VSA can view a range of behaviours through visual feedback such as:
behaviour while intoxicated; distressed appearance; himself talking
about sniffing behaviour; any of which can serve with the counsellor's
help to motivate the patient to want to change his behaviour and to
accept guidance to enable him to do so.   At a later stage VTR can be
used to record improvements as noted by the patient and fed back as an
index of improvement.

Suggestion Techniques

The importance of suggestion in the counselling relationship is
emphasised as a feature which underlies work from a wide range of
psychotherapies.   For example a factor common to all major divisions of
psychotherapy, such as Client Centred Psychotherapy (Rogers, 1952),
Behavioural Counselling (Krumboltz and Thoresen, 1969), and Gestalt
Therapy (Perls, 1972), is the suggestion implied or stated that the
patient's condition will improve as a result of the treatment.   In
medical cases undergoing drug therapy it has recently been observed
(Ashton, 1983), that some patients apparently experience no symptoms
when tranquilisers (benzodiazepines) are replaced by placebo.   Overall
it would seem to be that suggestion of a positive and directive kind is
the psychological ingredient underlying these counselling therapies.
It is interesting therefore to examine studies in which suggestion has
been specifically employed as a technique for the treatment of cases
presenting VSA problems.

Aversive Imagery Therapy

Aversion techniques as an extension of behaviour therapy have been applied in treatment for conditions such as alcoholism and sexual perversions (Rachman, 1965). A variation of this approach derives from the position that it is not desirable or necessary to use physical aversion techniques (e.g. chemical and/or electrical stimuli) with adolescents to inhibit problem behaviour. A method of deconditioning the unwanted behaviour by the use of noxious aversive stimuli at an imagery level is reported (Kolvin, 1967) in the treatment of a 'petrol addict', a boy of 15 years attending a school for the educationally subnormal. His main aversions concerned heights and falling which were employed as noxious stimuli in the following procedure. The patient was taken into a darkened room where he could relax with eyes closed in a lying position. The therapist then suggested a colourful story involving petrol sniffing which the patient was asked to visualise. When it became apparent that the patient was becoming affectively excited, the aversive image was introduced. The treatment proved to be effective, it involved twenty half-hour sessions undertaken on con-secutive days except for weekends. Thirteen months after treatment finished the patient was reported to be well and had not returned to his petrol sniffing habits.

More recently a style of aversion therapy used in conjunction with group counselling by a psychologist working with three teenage boys was reported (Lowenstein, 1982) in which the aversion therapy consisted of developing reactive inhibition by means of encouraging the boys to sniff until they became ill. The method reported seemed to rely heavily on the subject deciding volitionally to stop sniffing as an outcome of the group discussions.

In both of the strategies reported above it seems that a strong suggestion is made in the former it is implied in the latter study it is explicit, that VSA behaviour is bad and this suggestion is accepted by the person and on this basis the therapy proceeds. Whilst many patients are able to respond positively, depending upon the therapist's skill, to professional counselling utilising any one or more of a range of counselling techniques it is necessary to search for other methods which will offer the possibility of more effective treatment for those cases which do not respond easily to the basic therapies outlines above. Suggestive techniques can be used to advantage in various forms of counselling as shown above but perhaps the most significant indication of their value is when methods of hypnotherapy are employed.

Hypnotherapy

The application of hypnotic techniques to psychotherapy have been clearly stated by Hartland (1971) and Burrows and Dennerstein (1980). Current viewpoints on the subject hold that hypnosis can be used as an effective counselling tool to treat a wide range of problem behaviours (Ross, 1981). Waxman (1983) reviews the conflicting evidence on the efficacy of hypnosis in the treatment of substance abuses such as alcoholism and drug addiction and concludes that due to the many aetiological factors involved in these diseases it is unlikely that any one therapeutic approach will prove to be most effective. For example one of the principal factors involved seems to be the personality who suffers deep feelings of inadequacy and who is dependent on the chemical intoxication for emotional support. An eclectic approach is recommended in which hypnosis may contribute effectively in the short-term to the overall treatment. It seems probable that VSA cases may be viewed in a similar way.

Hypnotherapy presents new and interesting possibilities for treating chronic VSA patients who show strong resistance to conventional methods of therapy. The value of using hypnosis with discretion in the treatment of glue sniffing and solvent abuse has been indicated elsewhere by the author (O'Connor, 1982) and it is relevant here only to outline briefly the reasons why hypnotherapy can be useful in treating selected cases:

1. Susceptibility to suggestion aimed at behavioural change can be deepened by the induction of a trance state (Barber et al, 1974).

2. Many sniffers enjoy the experience of hallucinations while intoxicated which may render them more susceptible as subjects for imagery conditioning and behaviour modification through hypnosis. (Kroger and Fezler, 1976).

3. Hypnosis can be used as a quick short term treatment method of helping the VSA patient to:

   a. Reduce stress levels and relax.

   b. Feel better and gain self confidence because of the acceptance of ego-boosting suggestions made by the counsellor.

   c. Concentrate on ways of dealing positively with problems.

   d. Consider alternate means of gaining recreation, excitement and fulfilment.

Whilst the use of hypnosis with some VSA cases seems to offer the means whereby rapid improvements can be made it is necessary to add a cautionary note that treatments rarely prove effective in the long term unless adequate counselling attention is given to the underlying dynamic issues which appear to provoke severe sniffing behaviour.

From the foregoing the reader may well have gained the impression that hypnotherapy is a directive method of inducing change which is characterised by the giving of forceful commands to the patient. Whilst this can be an appropriate form to use with individual cases it is necessary to recognise that hypnotic techniques may be often used to their best advantage when a trance state is induced and the subject is given suggestions of calmness and relaxation and simply left to enjoy the benefits for a while until the therapist terminates the trance state. The main advantage of this method is that the patient can quickly be taught by this means to apply self hypnosis to overcome anxiety and panic attacks which can lead to the undesirable behaviour such as sniffing intoxicants.

A standard method of inducing hypnotic trance was used in which the patient was asked to stare fixedly at a point slightly above his head and to count backwards mentally from 250. During the induction period which sometimes lasted as long as four minutes the therapist made repeated low key suggestions of tiredness, dreaminess, drowsiness, relaxation and limpness. Once the trance had been induced deepening procedures were applied to increase the patient's suggestibility, for example, breathing to a slow rhythmic count, and raising and lowering the arms.

Therapy under hypnosis usually consisted in the following procedures:

1. Progressive relaxation of the body and mind to the degree where tension and stress were significantly lowered.

2. Ego strengthening and confidence building.

3. Ideomotor scanning to establish a communication link between the patient's unconscious and two of his fingers so that questions could be asked about the patient's feelings with regard to solvent inhalation and answered by a signal from the fingers to indicate yes or no.

4. Suggestions were made, which had been previously agreed with the client, regarding the gradual weaning away from and ending of the practice of glue sniffing and solvent abuse.

5. Elimination of negative feelings regarding the week ahead and reinforcement of happy, relaxed, positive attitudes to his self and his behaviour.

6. Removing the heightened suggestibility state and termination of the trance.

The reader is further advised that the use of hypnotherapy should take place only under the strictest professional control. Training courses in the use of hypnosis are organised for suitably qualified professionals by the British Society of Experimental and Clinical Hypnosis (BSECH) and by the British Society of Medical and Dental Hypnosis (BSMDH). Both of these societies advise a strict code of ethics in relation to the use of hypnosis with the protection of patients and therapists in mind.

Common Features of Effective Psychological Approaches

Effectiveness in treating VSA can be assessed in different ways. The primary aim is to stop the sniffing completely. But the success of treatment may also be measured in terms of reducing stress levels for individuals and helping them to develop through counselling improved skills of responding to problems. Effectiveness in the initial stages of treatment may be indicated by changes for the better in the way the individual feels about his life and predicament which may facilitate a gradual remission of the sniffing behaviour. Although treatment strategies for VSA are just beginning to be explored in response to

Department of Health and Social Security consultations on this subject (DHSS, 1983) there are already some common factors emerging from different successful approaches which merit consideration. For example, the importance of the factor of 'attentive listening' as a therapeutic strength in the counselling relationship with sniffers has already been mentioned and is referred to here again in a wider context.

Personal Attention

There would appear to be no single precipitating cause to account for any drug dependency and it would seem to be that in the case of VSA there are a multitude of causes and motives which result in individuals indulging chronic intake levels.* The common denominator in caring for such cases is meeting the individual and group needs for attention. Barnes (1979) refers to a study in USA by Rubin and Babbs (1970) evaluating different treatment approaches in dealing with glue sniffing in which the most success was achieved using a neighbourhood peer group with a probation counsellor assigned full time to the project. Special teachers were assigned to work with these boys for three hours each day. A significant feature of the treatment appeared to be that the families of boys were included in activities by both the counsellor and the teachers. Also, and most importantly the intensity of the treatment programme involved the boys in educational group recreational and counselling experiences day and night. A salient characteristic of the study referred to above which seems to be common to other successful treatment approaches to VSA is the amount of caring attention which is directed towards the sniffer from both family and caring professionals.

Approaches to treatment with this in mind will seek to train and educate the individual to make the most of life. Social and life skills training as promoted by the Schools Council and described by Hayes et al (1981) and specific advice on educational strategies to deal with solvent abuse by TACADE (1983) are indications of the ways in which VSA problems can be dealt with in the comprehensive schools at a prophylactic as well as therapeutic level. Recognition of VSA as a serious social problem has inspired many health education authorities to take action in ways already mentioned and which are motivated by a keen awareness that the problem cannot be allowed to remain unchecked.

Fundamentally though VSA remains a psychological problem. These noxious chemical vapours offer individuals a measure of emotional discharge and fulfilment which it is felt cannot be obtained in any other way. Effective treatments for the individual will have to provide the means whereby disabling emotional states for the young person such as frustration, depression, overexcitement, can be acted out in reality rather than internalised in phantasy. VSA seems to be in many ways a less threatening and less risky substitute for normal living.

*Chronic abuse refers to regular inhalation sessions occurring at least 4 days a week for a minimum of 3 hours a day.

The antidote lies in encouraging children and adolescents to learn how to live happily and fully through their own experiences. This task is beyond the treatment capabilities of the individual therapist alone. It is a long term management task which lies more within the province of the parents and teachers responsible for the child's development. Psychological approaches to the treatment of VSA have this in common: they seek to provide, albeit very often in a crisis situation, a substitute form of loving care and attention imbued with sensible discipline and guidance. The effectiveness of the treatment is conditional upon the degree to which the sniffer perceives sniffing as a habit he would like to stop and experiences the caring relationship as a healing process sufficiently strong to enable him to change his behaviour. It would seem therefore that the most effective approach to treatment of VSA is a multidisciplinary one. The ideal is for all the main child caring services including the Police Community Services to work as a team to make caring support for the young person and his family effective enough to overcome VSA practices in favour of health promoting activities which will keep the adolescent in touch with the real life of the community to which he belongs.

EMERGENCY TREATMENT

If a sniffer is found to be suffering any of the following: a state of collapse, incapacitating pains, e.g. in chest area, attacks of shaking and trembling or convulsions, semi-conscious state or coma, then the procedure should be to:

1. Remove the solvent product and materials including any plastic bag or rag especially if it is situated near the mouth and nose. Loosen clothing around the neck and chest to make breathing easier. If indoors open windows and doors to allow access to fresh air and ensure adequate ventilation.

2. Lie the person on his/her stomach with the head to the side to prevent vomit from being inhaled.

3. Cover the person with a blanket or coat to keep warm without hindering breathing.

4. Send for medical help or phone for an ambulance whichever is quicker and get the person to hospital as soon as possible. Retain the solvent and send to hospital with ambulance crew. If breathing has stopped commence mouth to mouth resuscitation immediately.

If the sniffer is high (intoxicated):

1. Remove solvent and bag.

2. Loosen tight clothing and ensure access to plenty fresh air.

3. Advise the person to breathe deeply and slowly.

4. If rapid breathing starts (hyperventilation) direct the person to breathe into a bag or cupped hands until breathing slows to normal.

5. Give nothing to drink or eat and stay with the person until he/she is fully conscious.

6. If possible inform parents and advise all concerned to seek professional guidance and help from:

    a. the family doctor or school health service.
    b. The school pastoral care team or the psychological guidance service.
    c. Social services.
    d. Voluntary counselling services.
    e. The local vicar or priest.

NB. The Police are always willing to send an officer from the community relations branch to advise youngsters and parents of the dangers of sniffing and how to get help.

7 OVERALL VIEW

Drugs have a universal appeal. Almost everyone uses drugs to some extent whether it is for medical reasons or in fulfilment of social expectations. Whatever the reasons for taking them drugs have the effect of making people feel better. It may be relief from a nagging headache or painful tooth, a sense of inferiority or a worry about loved ones, but the drugs people take will serve a function rather like a loyal servant upon whose services a person can become dependent. Drugs are now so much part of daily living patterns that there are drugs to fit every occasion and if they are available then why should they not be used?

This is the predicament of the young person who begins to dabble with sniffing intoxicating fumes. These potent chemicals are part of the social heritage young people are born into and they quickly learn that there are occasions on which it is useful to take drugs, e.g. when in pain, or depressed, or anxious, or in need of a mental uplift or just wanting to be in the fashion and appear agreeable. Intoxication through deliberately inhaling volatile vapours will perform any of these functions for the young person and if we ask why, what are the causes and the motivations for sniffing we become involved in a complexity of interlinked factors which criss cross with each other in unravelable permutations. It seems possible in this respect to state only that solvents and other volatiles are misused because they are available and have therefore the potential to perform a multitude of services for the sniffer. If therefore there is a situation in which a young person's feelings become distressed and disturbed glue sniffing will bring him temporary relief whereas another individual faced with the same kind of situation may choose not to sniff, but have other ways of finding relief. A lot depends on the individual's personality and attitudes to life as to whether the practice of solvent and volatile substance abuse will assume an incidental or a dominant role in his behaviour.

When for whatever reasons a young person decides that his sniffing activities have reached intolerable proportions he will probably need help to make the change from a sniffing to a non sniffing behaviour routine. It is at this stage that the individual's motives for sniffing and factors in the background which may have caused undue stress become important in consideration of the treatment strategies which might effectively be applied in each case.

93

For example it is currently observed (G.P., 1983) that the premorbid personality of the drug user is often linked with psychiatric or emotional problems. Additionally it is thought that the drugs themselves can potentially induce psychiatric disturbances which has already been observed with VSA by Glaser (1966) who first applied the term 'Inhalation Psychosis'. Dependency on drugs can lead to psychopathological changes whereby the drug user sees himself as a weak person unable to control his habit and this is certainly the case with many of the sniffers attending the Clinic who said they hated themselves for stealing to satisfy their cravings for solvents. Over the last two years four teenage girls attending the Clinic, all in care at CHE's, reported having resorted to prostitution at times to finance their needs for substances to sniff. Often the sniffer develops a tough image to disguise his vulnerability. Also some cases reported not eating for several days or mentioned that they tended to survive on commercial foods (noted earlier in the text), such as burgers, chips, milk, chocolate bars, boiled sweets etc. Vitamin deficiencies and dietary imbalances have often been observed with cases at the Clinic as possibly causing skin complaints and in girls menstruation problems.

In relation to the provision of treatment for sniffers who want to stop the question arises as to how far society has an obligation to intervene and legislate on the availability of these chemicals for use by the young.

In this respect it is significant that police intervention with glue sniffers has usually involved a caring role. Youngsters intoxicated by solvent vapours often need protection from the accidental outcomes or the physiological ill effects and the police have often had to intervene to help the person and sometimes to save lives. In view of this it is not surprising that professional concern for the welfare of the young and public alarm at the dangers of solvent abuse have caused demands in Parliament for legislation.

Many questions have been asked in the Houses of Parliament regarding the urgency of finding appropriate measures with which to control the sale of products containing volatile substances to young people. Of all the parliamentary questions and answers referring to volatile substance abuse the following extract from Hansard for 14th December 1981 is typical. The question was asked by Baroness Phillips in the House of Lords:

'To ask Her Majesty's Government whether they will introduce regulations to control the sale of 'glue sniffing' solvents to young people?'

The reply, by Lord Lyell, expresses the apparent helplessness of the would be legislator:

'My Lords, there are no powers under consumer safety legislation to control the sale of glue sniffing solvents to young people, but even if there were the Government would consider their use unjustified. There is a very wide range of what we call 'sniffable' solvents and of shops that sell them. Enforcement of a ban or other controls would probably prove ineffective and it would be hard to justify any age limit.'

In a consultative paper dated 18th January 1983 the Department of Health and Social Security sought advice on the problem posed, largely to young people, by solvent abuse.   Of necessity the main response to this problem will be a social one in terms of how far local communities are able to contain and control the behaviour of young people intoxicated by solvents.   Unlike drink and drugs there does not seem to be a feasible method of implementing controls by statute on the supply of volatile substances misused by sniffers.   Increasingly young people are to be found on the streets behaving under the influence of solvent intoxication or actually glue sniffing in public places and there is virtually nothing that can be done about them.   In this connection there is a relevant section of the Children and Young Persons' Act 1969 S.28(2) which could be used to empower a constable to detain without warrant any juvenile in respect of whom he has reasonable cause to believe that the following condition is satisfied, viz.

'his proper development is being avoidably prevented or neglected or his health is being avoidably impaired or neglected'.

But further considerations arise.   There is enough evidence of a scientific and clinical nature (Volans, 1982) to justify the conclusion that glue sniffing practices are potentially dangerous and when carried out in public are a bad example to other children as well as being objectionable to the public at large.   There is a need for the right to detain a child or young teenager in police custody for long enough to enable enquiries to be made regarding the extent to which this person is at risk through sniffing activities.   Otherwise we are faced with the situation in which young people are being allowed by default to place themselves at great risk by inhaling poisonous fumes to hazardous levels. The following case taken from Halsburys Laws of England Review for November 1982 serves as a prime example to illustrate the dilemma which needs to be resolved.

Youth aged 16, no previous convictions.   Taken into care in 1980 as a result of a period in hospital for sniffing glue.   Parents would not have him at home.   Went onto motorway bridge with another youth and threw rocks down to watch passing cars swerve. Appellant dropped a rock which went through a car windscreen and killed a passenger.   Sentenced to 6 years detention for manslaughter.   On appeal held because of personal antecedents and reports before the Court the sentence would be reduced to 3 years detention.   This should not be taken as setting any sort of tariff for the sentence to be expected by anybody who engages in this wicked and dangerous pastime.   R. -v- Larkin, 8th July, 1982 (Court of Appeal: O'Connor L.J. and Purchas,J.)

In Scotland appropriate action has already been taken by means of the new Solvent Abuse (Scotland) Act 1983 which adds solvent abuse to the conditions indicating the need for a compulsory care order and giving the police powers to intervene and detain young people at risk. Similar legislation is under consideration for other areas of the UK but whatever the outcomes of the proposals may be they can at least show that Government is fulfilling its responsibility to protect and care for all who fall within its jurisdiction.   This responsibility is especially necessary with regard to the young who are the future

strength of the community.   What is needed is some guidance from
society as to what constitutes right and wrong behaviour.   Legislation
which sets out to limit the availability of volatile substances to young
people would at least indicate that society cares sufficiently about the
young to advise them strongly against indulging practices which have the
potential to injure and cause death.   It would do the young people of
our culture no harm, and it might do some good, to at least hear the
Voice of society's conscience in relation to these self inflicted
abuses.

The prospects for the future are bleak if no attempt is made to
control the abuse by the young of volatile substances.   Throughout this
book there are references to the suffering that can be caused for the
person by VSA which is testimony to the need for caring interventions in
the lives of children and teenagers who are at risk by having free
access to intoxicating substances.   The problem of Volatile Substance
Abuse by the young shows no sign of going away which means that one way
or another some of us will have to care for the sniffers in need.   This
book is primarily intended to help those who would willingly share this
caring responsibility despite the indifference and even hostility to the
notion which is shown by others.

8 POSTSCRIPT

It was Easter weekend and everyone was enjoying the holiday. The
Bridge Yard Punk Group had been on a sniffing binge since Friday night.
By Monday morning most of the group had dispersed leaving only five hard
core sniffers. The two girls Nicola and Liz were still working the
best out of a 2 litre tin of paint while the boys, Greg, Andy and Eric
were on thinners. By 10.00 o'clock they had just about had enough and
began to move up from the copse by the dual carriageway towards the
small shopping centre situated within easy reach of three massive tower
blocks. The mood of the group was mischievous bordering on the ugly as
they began to experience the first downbeats of the inevitable hangover.
As they passed the entrance to Barkside Court they indulged in a stone
throwing session which smashed the toilet window of a corner flat.
Some recently planted flowering trees were uprooted and broken scatter-
ing soil over the pavement areas. When they reached the shopping
square they were yelling a lot and generally roughhousing each other.
Suddenly into their midst walked 4 yr old Robert Agnew wearing his new
Easter suit. The details of what happened next are not precisely known
because Robert is still unable to speak easily about the incident but an
old age pensioner watched the scene from a third floor tower flat:

> 'I thought they were playing with a big doll or Guy Fawkes dummy,
> he said. They were tossing it from one to the other, then they
> poured paint over it and started stripping away some of the
> clothes. It was only later I found out it was a child they'd
> been molesting.'

When Robert's mother saw him she could not believe her eyes. He was
smeared from head to foot with lilac coloured paint and his new clothes
were ruined. She lost her temper and began to hit out screaming at him
for getting into such a state when he had gone out to play barely
minutes before with a warning not to get dirty. She said afterwards
that it was only after her first reaction began to subside that she
realised he could hardly breathe for the paint around his mouth:

> 'It was when he did not cry I knew something was wrong. He
> was all stiff and breathing queer. He kept trying to wipe
> away the paint from his face and he looked absolutely scared
> stiff. He was petrified.'

Only the names of some people and places have been changed in this
account to preserve confidentiality for those who were hurt most by it.
Robert developed breathing problems which necessitated hospital and
drugs to regularise his breathing.   For days afterwards he suffered the
shock effects of the experience and all the terror he'd felt but not
expressed at the time came out in the weeks that followed.   He now
'wets the bed most nights' and refuses to play alone outside.   He
suffers nightmares about glue sniffers and cannot bear to sleep without
a light during the night.   His health deteriorated so much that his
mother applied to the local authority for another council house and was
given medical certificates describing Robert's health to support her
application.   Unfortunately two weeks after moving into her new house
it was burgled and Robert harbours the idea that it was the 'sniffers
come back to get him'.

There are many similar incidents to the above which are never recorded
in the official statistics so much revered of government departments.
No individual was ever charged with an offence following the assault on
Robert.   The youths concerned although their identities were known were
never punished in any way or made to feel by official action that what
they had done was wrong.   It is only when we examine individual cases
such as the above that the ill effects on the community of behaviour
triggered by sniffing intoxicants is fully realised.   The cost in terms
of human misery and suffering is highlighted by episodes such as the one
involving Robert which leads to the question of at what cost do we
maintain a low profile approach to problems of glue sniffing and solvent
abuse only to reinforce uncaring attitudes and lack of social response.
No doubt the charge of emotional overstatement can be made when there is
reference to individual cases of hardship and suffering.   This is a
device frequently employed to buffer the sensitivities of the professional caring services for economic reasons.   To advocate a policy of
non intervention would be to fail to recognise the existence of a
problem at all.   Such a manoeuvre would be a 'cop out' of major
proportions.   The alternative is to pursue an humanitarian approach
incorporating principles in which everyone has the responsibility of
caring for his neighbour as well as the right to be cared for.   In this
respect caring is a supreme act of goodwill to all but especially to
those mostly in need.   A statement from a related context (Henrikson,
1983) is relevant to the need for an effective response to volatile
substance abuse by young people:

'The most expensive solution of all would be to do nothing'.

9 REFERENCES

AA. Leaflet: <u>A Message to Teenagers</u>, Alcoholics Anonymous, London, 1982.

AMCOR, <u>Information Relating to the Modulon Air Ioniser</u>, Roncastle, London Ltd., 1981

Anderson, H.R., Dick, B., MacNair, R.S., Palmer, J.C., and Ramsey, J.D., An Investigation of 140 Deaths associated with Volatile Substance Abuse in the United Kingdom (1971-1981). <u>J.Human Toxicology</u> 1,3, 207-221. 1982

Ashton, Dr.Heather C. Benzodiazepine Dependence and Withdrawal. <u>Pharmacology Newsletter</u>, Published by Regional Drug Information Service and Regional Clinical Pharmacology Unit, April 1983.

Ashton*, M.,Poisons Unit Symposium on Solvent Abuse, <u>Druglink</u>, Spring ISDD, p.p. 6-9, 1983

Barber, T.X., Spanos, H.P., and Chaves, J.F., <u>Hypnosis, Imagination and Human Potential</u>, Pergamon Press, New York, 1974

Barker, G. and Adams, W., Glue Sniffers, <u>Sociology and Social Res</u> 47,(3), 298-310, 1963.

Barnes, G.E., Solvent Abuse: A Review, <u>Int.J.Addictions</u> 14(1) 1-26, 1979.

Bass, M., Sudden Sniffing Death, <u>J.Am.Med.Assoc.</u> 212(12) 2075-2079, 1970.

Berger, M.M., <u>Videotape Techniques in Psychiatric Training and Treatment</u>, Brunner/Mazel, N.Y. 1978.

Black, D., Misuse of Solvents, <u>DHSS Paper</u>, HMSO, 1982

Boecks, R. and Goodin, F., An Epidemic of Gasoline Sniffing. <u>Paper Presented to 1st Int.Symposium on Deliberate Inhalation of Industrial Solvents</u>, Mexico City, 1976

Brecher, E.M., <u>Licit and Illicit Drugs</u>, Consumers' Union: N.Y. 1972

Brozovsky, M. and Winkler, E.G., Glue Sniffing in Children and Adolescents. <u>N.Y. State J.Med.</u> 65, 1984-1989, 1965

Burrows, G.D., and Dennerstein, C., (Editors). <u>Handbook of Hypnosis and Psychosomatic Medicine</u>, North Holland: Elsevier, Oxford Biomedical Press, 1980.

Clark, D.G., and Tinston, D.J., Correlations of the Cardiac Sensitising Potential of Halogenated Hydrocarbons with their Physiochemical Properties. <u>B.J.Pharmacol</u>. 49, 355-357, 1973

Clements, J.E., and Simpson, R., Environmental and Behavioural Aspects of Glue Sniffing in a Population of Emotionally Disturbed Adolescents, <u>Int.J.Addict</u>. 13(1) 129-134, 1978

Cohen, S., The Drug Dilemma, McGraw-Hill, N.Y.,1969.

Cohen, S., Inhalant Abuse: An Overview of the Problem, Nat.Inst.Drug Abuse Res.Monog.Series 15, 2-11, 1977

Comstock, E.G., and Comstock, B.S., Medical Evaluation of Inhalant Abusers, Nat.Inst.Drug Abuse Res.Monog.Ser. 15, 54-80, 1977

Corliss, L.M., A Review of the Evidence on Glue Sniffing: A Persistent Problem. J.Schl.Health, 35. 442-449, 1965

Cross, H.J., and Kelinhesselink, R.R., Psychological Perspectives on Drugs and Youth. In Ch.14. Haviland, J. and Scarborough, H., Adolescent Development in Contemporary Society D.Van Norstrand Co., 1981, N.Y. 1980.

Curtis, L., Glue Sniffing: Big Trouble in a Tube, Bureau of Naval Personnel, Navy Dept., USA, 1968.

D'Amanda, C., Plumb, M.M., and Taintor, Z., Heroin Addicts with a History of Glue Sniffing: A Deviant Group within a Deviant Group Int.J.Addictions, 12(2-3) 255-270, 1977.

DHSS, Information Documents on Solvent Misuse (Glue Sniffing), Margaret Pearson, Community Services Division, 1983

Drug Liaison Group, Solvent Vapour Inhalation (Glue Sniffing): Notes for Professionals in Child Care, Newcastle upon Tyne Area Health Authority (Teaching), 1981.

Effron, D., Holmstedt, B., and Kline, N., Ethnographic Search for Psycho-active Drugs. Public Health Safety Publications, No.1645, US Gov.Printing Office, Washington DC 20402, 1967.

Francis, J., Murray, V.S.G., Ruprah, M., Flanagan, R.J., and Ramsey,J.D. Suspected Solvent Abuse in Cases Referred to the Poisons Unit, Guy's Hospital, July 1980 - June 1981. J.Human Toxicology, 1,(3) 271-280, 1982.

Gay, M., Mellor, R., and Stanley, S., Drug Abuse Monitoring: A Survey of Solvent Abuse in the County of Avon. J.Human Toxicology 1(3) 257-264, 1982.

Glaser, F.B., Inhalation Psychosis and Related States. Archives of General Psychiatry 14, 315-322, 1966.

Glaser, H.H., and Massengale, O.N., Glue Sniffing in Children. J.Am. Med.Assoc. 181(4) 300-303, 1962.

G.P. Drug Abuse, Pull Out Supplement, General Practitioner 25th March 1983.

Grabski, D.A., Toluene Sniffing Producing Cerebellar Degeneration Am.J.Psychiat. 118, 461-462, 1961.

Hartland, J., Medical and Dental Hypnosis and Its Clinical Applications 2nd Ed. Baillier-Tindal, London, 1971.

Hayes, B., Sluckin, A., and Smith, A., Social Skills Course in a Comprehensive School Curriculum. Schools Council, 1981.

Hertzberg, J.L., and Wolkind, S.N., Solvent Sniffing in Perspective. B.J. Hospital Medicine, January 1983

Henrikson, B., Review of Swedish Youth Council Report; 'Not for Sale' Guardian Newspaper, March 23rd, 1983.

ISDD, The Deliberate Inhalation of Volatile Substances. (STASH) Student Association for Study of Hallucinogens, Inc. Wisconsin, USA. 1974.

ISDD, Teaching About a Volatile Situation, Institute for the Study of Drug Dependence, London, July 1980.

Jamieson, J.H., All Buzzed Up, Community Homes Gazette, 74, 171-174 1980

Kerr, M., Education v Legislation. The Police Review, 14,12,1979
King, M.D., Neurological Sequelae of Toluene Abuse. J.Human Toxicology
  3(1) 281-288, 1982
Knox, J.W., and Nelson, J.R., Permanent Encephalopathy from Toluene
  Inhalation. N.Eng.J.Med. 275, 1494-1496, 1966
Kolvin, I., Aversive Imagery Treatment in Adolescence. Behaviour
  Research and Therapy 5,245-248, 1967
Krasowski, J., A Psychosocial Theory of Solvent Abusers. Drug Forum
  7 (3 & 4) 1978-79, 371-382. Baywood Pub.Co.Inc. (USA) 1979
Kroeger, R.M., Moore, R.J., Lehman, T.H., Giesy, J.D., and Skeeters,C.E.,
  Recurrent Urinary Calculi Associated with Toluene Sniffing.
  J. Urology, 123, 89-90, 1980
Kroger, W.S., and Fezler, W.D., Hypnosis and Behaviour Modification
  Imagery Conditioning. Philadelphia. J.B. Lippincott Co., 1976.
Krug, S.E., and Henry, T.J., Personality, Motivation and Adolescent
  Drug Abuse Patterns. J. Counselling Psychol. 21(5) 440-445, 1974
Krumboltz, J.D., and Thoresen, C.E., Behavioural Counselling: Cases
  and Techniques, Holt, Rhinehart and Winston, 1969
Kupperstein, L.R. and Susman, R.M., A Bibliography on the Inhalation of
  Glue Fumes and Other Toxic Vapours. Int.J.Addict. 3(1) 1968
Lewis, P., and Patterson, D.W., Acute and Chronic Effects of the
  Voluntary Inhalation of Certain Commercial Volatile Solvents by
  Juveniles. J.Drug Issues. 4(2) 162-175, 1974
Lombroso, C. and Lerman, P., Breath holding spells (Cyanotic and
  Pallid Infantile Syncope) Pediatrics, 29(4) 1967
Lowenstein, L.F. , Glue Sniffing: Background Features and Treatment by
  Aversion Methods and Group Therapy. The Practitioner, 226, 1113-1116,
  1982
Massengale, O., Glaser, H., Lelievre, R., Dodds, J., and Klock, M.,
  Physical and Psychological Factors in Glue Sniffing. N.Eng.J.Med.
  269, 1340-1344, 1963
Masterton, G., The Management of Solvent Abuse. J. Adolescence 2, 65-
  75, 1979
McMaster, J. McG., (Editor), Methods in Social and Educational Caring
  Gower Pub.Co.Ltd., 1982
Merrill, E., Problems of Children Stuck on Glue, Community Care
  12.7.1978.
Montaigne, M., Essays (translated by J.M. Cohen). Penguin Books Ltd.,
  Bk.I LV. London, 1958
Nurcombe, B., Bianchi, G., Money, J., and Cawte, J., A Hunger for
  Stimuli. B.J.Med.Psych. 43(4) 367-374. 1970
O'Connor, D.J., A Profile of Solvent Abuse in Schoolchildren. J.Child.
  Psychol.Psychiat. 20, 365-368, 1979
O'Connor, D.J. The Glue Sniffing Craze: Researching the Facts from
  Case Studies. DHSS, HMSO Social Work Service Magazine 27, 5-10 1981.
O'Connor, D.J., The Use of Suggestion Techniques with Adolescents in
  the Treatment of Glue Sniffing and Solvent Abuse. J.Human Toxicology
  1, (3) 313-320, 1982
O'Connor, D.J., Research Report: Glue Sniffing and the Abuse of
  Solvents by Schoolchildren and Adolescents. Durham and Newcastle Res.
  Rev. X(50) 1983
Oswald, I., Sleep. Pelican Books, London, 1966

Peers, I., Dealing with Solvent Misuse p.25. TACADE Publication,
    2 Mount Street, Manchester. 1983
Perls, F.S., Gestalt Therapy Verbatim, Bantam Books, 1972.
Pickens, R.W., and Heston, L.L. (Editors). Psychiatric Factors in Drug
    Abuse, Grune and Stratton, N.Y., 1979
Pink Floyd. Song: 'We don't want no education'. Pink Floyd Music Group
    1980
Plant, M., Drug Takers in an English Town, Tavistock, London. 1975
Preble, E., and Laury, G.V., Plastic Cement: The Ten Cent Hallucinogen.
    Int.J. Addictions,2(2) 1967
Press, E., and Done, A.K., Solvent Sniffing. Pediatrics 39(3) 451-461
    and 39(4) 611-621
Rachman, S., Aversion Therapy: Chemical or Electrical. Behav.Res.
    and Therapy 2,289-300, 1965
Roberts, D.J., Abuse of Aerosol Products by Inhalation, Human
    Toxicology 1, 3, 231-238, 1982
Robins and Cohen, Knuckle Sandwich, Pelican, p.151. London 1978.
Robinson, R.O., Tetraethyl Lead Poisoning from Gasoline Sniffing.
    J.American Med.Assoc. 240(13) 1373-1376. 1978
Rogers, C.R., Client Centred Psychotherapy. The Scientific American
    Nov. 1952
Ross, P.J., Hypnosis as a Counselling Tool. B.J. Guidance and
    Counselling 9(2) 173-179. 1981
Rubin, T. and Babbs, J., The Glue Sniffer. Fed.Probation 34: 23-28
    1970
Sasa, M., Igarashi, S., Miyazaki, T., Miyasaki, K., Nakono, S., and
    Matsuko, I., Equilibrium Disorders with Diffuse Brain Atrophy in
    Long Term Toluene Sniffing. Arch. Otohinolaryngol 221, 163-169.1978.
Scholtes, M.H., and Senior,C.A.,Sniffing it/Snuffing it. Hope Press
    Publications, London 1983.
Schottstaedt, M.F., and Bjork,J.W.Inhalant Abuse in an Indian Boarding
    School. Am.J.Psychiat. 134(11) 1290-1293. 1977
Shorter, E. The Making of the Modern Family. Basic Books, London,1975.
Silberberg, N.E., and Silberberg, M.C., Glue Sniffing: A Position
    Paper. J.Drug.Ed. 4 (3). 301-307. 1976
Skuse, D. and Burrell, S., A Review of Solvent Abusers and their
    management by a Child Psychiatric Out-Patient. J.Human Toxicology
    1982
Smith, H., Inhalation of Volatile Substances. The Pharmchem.Newsletter
    5(2) Feb. 1976.
Sokol, J., Glue Sniffing among Juveniles. Am.J.Corrections 27: 18-21
    1965
STASH, The Deliberate Inhalation of Volatile Substances. Student
    Association for the Study of Hallucinogens, inc. STASH Press
    Winsconsin. 1974
Strathclyde Regional Council. Solvent Abuse: A Corporate Approach.
    Social Work Dept., Glasgow, G.2. 1982
Swedish Board of Health and Welfare, Stockholm. Actions against
    Sniffing Swedish Gov.Publication. 1978
TACADE (Peers, I.S.) Dealing with Solvent Abuse, TACADE. London. 1983
Towfighi, J., Gonatas, N., Pleasure, D., Cooper, H.S., and McCree, L.,
    Glue Sniffers Neuropathy. Neurology 26, 238-243. 1976
UN Narcotics Information - Mexico. Abuse of Inhalable Volatile
    Substances Information Letter. UN Division of Narcotic Drugs. NY.
    1977

Watson, L.M., The Management of Drug Abuse in School Children. <u>Pub.</u> <u>Hlth</u>. London 86, 10-19. 1972

Watson, J.M., Solvent Sniffing. <u>Strathclyde Police Guardian</u> 6: 65-66 1976

Watson, J.M., Glue Sniffing: A Community Dilemma. <u>Community Health</u> 8(3) 161-163, 1977

Watson, J.M., Clinical and Laboratory Investigations in 132 cases of Solvent Abuse. <u>Med.Sci.Law</u> 18(1) 40-43. 1978

Watson, J.M., Morbidity and Mortality Statistics. <u>Med.Sci.Law</u> 19,4 246-252, 1979.

Watson, J.M., Solvent Abuse: Presentation and Clinical Diagnosis <u>J.Human Toxicology</u> 1 (3) 249-256, 1982

Waxman, D., The Treatment of Alcohol and Drug Addiction: An Overview <u>9th Int.Congr. of Hypnosis and Psychosomatic Medicine. Conference</u> <u>Report</u> 1983

Will, A.M., and MacLaren, E.H., Reversible Renal Shutdown <u>British</u> <u>Medical Journal</u> 283, 525-526. 1981

Wyse, D.G., Deliberate Inhalation of Volatile Hydrocarbons: A Review <u>Canad.Med.Ass.J.</u> 108 71-74. 1973